Easy to Use

PICK UP & PLAY

SCALES
for Great SOLOS

SEE IT ■ HEAR IT

ALAN BROWN   JAKE JACKSON

Flame Tree
Music

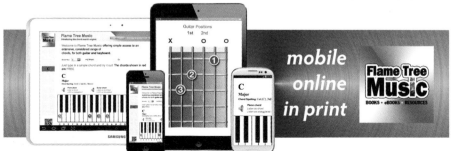

mobile
online
in print

Flame Tree
Music
BOOKS ■ eBOOKS ■ RESOURCES

Contents

Publisher/Creative Director: Nick Wells • Layout Design: Jane Ashley • Website and Software: David Neville with Stevens Dumpala and Steve Moulton • Editorial: Gillian Whitaker

First published 2017 by
FLAME TREE PUBLISHING
6 Melbray Mews, Fulham,
London SW6 3NS, United Kingdom
flametreepublishing.com

Music information site: flametreemusic.com

18 19 20 21 22 23 • 2 3 4 5 6 7 8 9 10

© 2017 Flame Tree Publishing Ltd

The CIP record for this book is available from the British Library.

ISBN: 978-1-78664-554-8

All images and notation courtesy of Flame Tree Publishing Ltd, except the following: guitar diagrams © 2017 Jake Jackson/Flame Tree Publishing Ltd. Courtesy of Shutterstock.com and copyright the following photographers: Ronald Sumners 10; Elnur 14; Anton_Ivanov 18; Miguel Garcia Saavedra 23; Roman Voloshyn 26; Syda Productions 31; Pavel L Photo and Video 36; Simone Conti 39; Africa Studio 41.

Every effort has been made to contact copyright holders. We apologize in advance for any omissions and would be pleased to insert the appropriate acknowledgement in subsequent editions of this publication.

Android is a trademark of Google Inc. Logic Pro, iPhone and iPad are either registered trademarks or trademarks of Apple Computer Inc. in the United States and/or other countries. Cubase is a registered trademark or trademark of Steinberg Media Technologies GmbH, a wholly owned subsidiary of Yamaha Corporation, in the United States and/or other countries. Nokia's product names are either trademarks or registered trademarks of Nokia. Nokia is a registered trademark of Nokia Corporation in the United States and/or other countries. Samsung and Galaxy S are both registered trademarks of Samsung Electronics America, Ltd. in the United States and/or other countries.

This book uses material adapted from *Scales and Modes* by Alan Brown & Jake Jackson, originally published in 2009.

Alan Brown (musical examples) is a former member of the Scottish National Orchestra. He now works as a freelance musician with several leading UK orchestras, and as a consultant in music and IT. Alan has had several compositions published, developed a set of music theory CD-Roms, co-written a series of bass guitar examination handbooks and worked on over 100 further titles.

Jake Jackson (author) is a writer and musician. He has created and contributed to over 25 practical music books, including *Guitar Chords* and *How to Play Guitar*. His music is available on iTunes, Amazon and Spotify amongst others.

Printed in China

Scales for Great Solos
An Introduction

For creative music making, either composition or improvisation, the more scales in more keys that you know, the greater will be your flexibility and expressive capabilities. In this book, you'll find:

1. The scales most commonly used for solo improvisation, divided by key. Each scale is shown ascending and descending, in both traditional and TAB notation, with a few chords they work well with included at the top.

2. A section on the basic theory behind scales, outlining their relationship to keys, chords and composition.

3. The scale formations behind the most common types of scales, as well as some less common scale types, so that you can apply their patterns to any key for further experimentation.

4. Advice on constructing solos, with some examples of scales in use for this purpose. Mentions of scales favoured by particular artists are also dotted throughout, as well as the scale types best for various music styles.

5. QR code links to **flametreemusic.com**, allowing you to find your way quickly to the scale you want, work out what to play, and hear the scale online. An extensive library of chords is also available there.

Understanding the relationship of notes to one another in a key is one of the greatest ways to develop as a muscian. When it comes to solos, if you build up a knowledge-base of scales, you will be able to play around with a huge variety of sounds with ease and expertise. We hope this book will provide musicians of all levels with a solid point of reference that can be used to enhance music-making of all kinds.

START
HERE

BASICS

A

A♯/B♭

B

C

C♯/D♭

D

D♯/E♭

E

F

F♯/G♭

G

G♯/A♭

The Diagrams
A Quick Guide

Each scale is notated in both traditional musical notation and guitar tablature. This book assumes some musical knowledge, although below diagrams are for reference.

Standard Notation

C C♯ D D♯ E F F♯ G G♯ A A♯ B

TAB Notation

Some guitarists prefer to use tablature (called TAB) instead of staves. The six lines represent the six strings of the guitar, from the high E string to the low E string, and the numbers represent the frets that produce the notes. A zero indicates that the string is played open. In the below example, the first C is played on the 5th string – the A string – by holding down the third fret along.

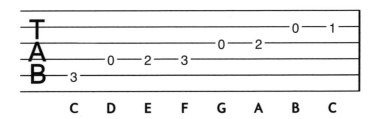

C   D   E   F   G   A   B   C

FREE ACCESS on iPhone & Android etc, using any free QR code app

Scan to **HEAR** the C major chord, and access the full library of scales and chords on flametreemusic.com

The Fretboard

With scales, it's helpful to have a clear idea of where each note lies in relation to other notes. On the guitar, the frets are organized in semitone intervals.

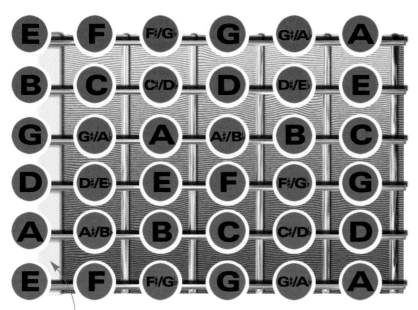

For a labelled diagram of notes on a keyboard, see page 8.

Nut

Tones and Semitones

The scale patterns in this book are described in terms of the letters 'T' and 'S':

T T S T T T S

S = Semitone (USA half-step)   **T** = Tone (USA whole step)

A semitone (or half-step) is the smallest musical interval in Western music, and a tone is equal to two semitones. See pages 8-9 for more on scale formation.

Scan to **HEAR** the C major chord, and access the full library of scales and chords on flametreemusic.com

START HERE

BASICS

A

A♯/B♭

B

C

C♯/D♭

D

D♯/E♭

E

F

F♯/G♭

G

G♯/A♭

START
HERE

BASICS

A

A♯/B♭

B

C

C♯/D♭

D

D♯/E♭

E

F

F♯/G♭

G

G♯/A♭

The Sound Links
Another Quick Guide

Requirements: a camera and internet-ready smartphone (e.g. **iPhone**, any **Android** phone (e.g. **Samsung Galaxy**), **Nokia Lumia**, or **camera-enabled tablet** such as the **iPad Mini**). The best result is achieved using a WIFI connection.

1. Download any **free QR code reader**. An app store search will reveal a great many of these, so obviously it's best to go with the ones with the highest ratings and don't be afraid to try a few before you settle on the one that works best for you. Tapmedia's QR Reader app is good, or ATT Scanner (used below) or QR Media. Some of the free apps have ads, which can be annoying.

2. On your smartphone, open the app and **scan** the **QR code** at the base of any particular page.

FREE ACCESS on iPhone & Android etc, using any free QR code app

Scan to HEAR the C major chord, and access the full library of scales and chords on flametreemusic.com

7

3. For the scales section, each code at the bottom of the page will bring you to the relevant scale on flametreemusic.com. Scanning the code on all other pages will bring you to the C major chord, and from there you can access and hear the complete library of scales and chords.

FREE ACCESS on iPhone & Android etc, using any free QR code app

Scan to HEAR the C major chord, and access the full library of scales and chords on flametreemusic.com

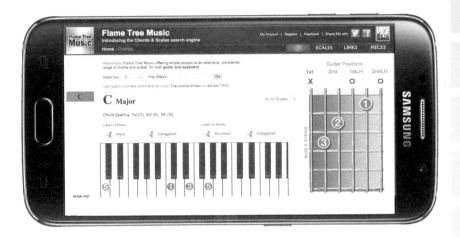

4. Use the drop down menu to choose from **20 scales** or 12 **free chords** (50 with subscription) per key.

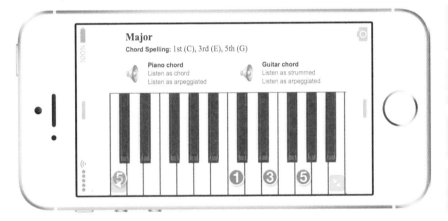

5. Click the sounds! Both piano and guitar audio is provided. This is particularly helpful when you're playing with others.

The QR codes give you direct access to chords and scales. You can access a much wider range of chords if you register and subscribe.

FREE ACCESS on iPhone & Android etc, using any free QR code app

Scan to **HEAR** the C major chord, and access the full library of scales and chords on flametreemusic.com

START
HERE

BASICS

A

A#/B♭

B

C

C#/D♭

D

D#/E♭

E

F

F#/G♭

G

G#/A♭

What are Scales?

A scale is a set of ordered pitches. Different scales produce different tonalities, but they follow patterns that can be applied to each key.

Formation of a Scale

For each of the scales included in this book, we have included the scale pattern. This shows the **relationship** between each note in the scale. For example, the scale pattern of the major scale is:

T T S T T T S

It can help to picture these intervals on a piano keyboard, like the one below.

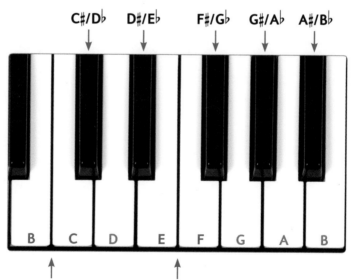

Semitone interval between these notes

FREE ACCESS on iPhone & Android etc, using any free QR code app

Scan to **HEAR** the C major chord, and access the full library of scales and chords on flametreemusic.com

An **interval** is the distance between two pitches. As such:

B to C = one semitone
C to C♯ = one semitone
C to D = one tone (or two semitones)

We can apply the **major scale pattern** to the key of C, to produce the **C Major scale.** Starting with C, a tone from C is D, then a tone from D is E, then a semitone from E is F, and so on. So using the scale pattern opposite in C Major produces the following notes:

C D E F G A B C

On the keyboard, the C Major scale only uses the white notes.

Other Intervals

Some scale spellings include other interval names, such as **m3** and **a2**. Both of these are the equivalent of 3 semitones: m3 means '**minor 3d**', and a2 refers to '**augmented 2nd**'.

The **C Major Pentatonic scale**, for example, is a mix of tones and minor 3rds. it consists of the following notes, with the pattern shown below:

C D E G A C
T   T   m3   T   m3

Using the piano diagram opposite, you can see that the distance between E and G involves 3 steps, making that minor 3rd interval.

Scan to **HEAR** the C major chord, and access the full library of scales and chords on flametreemusic.com

START
HERE

BASICS

A

A#/Bb

B

C

C#/Db

D

D#/Eb

E

F

F#/Gb

G

G#/Ab

FREE ACCESS on iPhone & Android
etc, using any free QR code app

Scan to **HEAR** the C major chord, and
access the full library of scales and
chords on flametreemusic.com

The Scale-Key-Chord Relationship

The **harmonic links** that exist between notes are central to understanding which notes will sound good together, and which won't. Being able to recognize the relationship between notes will improve your playing technique as well as give you the knowledge to compose your own music.

A scale orders the notes of a key by **pitch**. It is common to number notes in a scale using Roman numerals, so the scale of C major could be written as:

C	D	E	F	G	A	B
I	II	III	IV	V	VI	VII
1st	2nd	3rd	4th	5th	6th	7th

The **position** of a note in a scale alerts you to its importance. For example, the first degree (the '**tonic**') is usually central to estabilishing the tonality of a section of music. The V note (the '**dominant**') is also important due to its strong harmonic relationship with the tonic (i.e. G is closely linked to C here).

Chords derived from these seven notes would all be using notes from the C major scale. So, if you were given the chord **Cmaj7**, which comprises the notes **C, E, G and B**, soloing with the C major scale wouldn't sound out of place. As such, when choosing **compatible** scales and chords, it helps to know how they relate to the overall key.

The right choice of scale for a group of chords often depends on the context, as there can be many options that produce different effects. We've included some chord **suggestions** in the scale section of this book though.

FREE ACCESS on iPhone & Android etc, using any free QR code app

Scan to **HEAR** the C major chord, and access the full library of scales and chords on flametreemusic.com

Modes

START
HERE

Most scales can be recycled to generate more scales with different interval structures and therefore different sounds, simply by starting the new scale on each degree of the old scale. An example is the set of **major scale modes**, which appear in several groups:

- **Dorian:** contains the notes of the major scale starting from its second degree.

- **Phrygian:** contains the notes of the major scale starting from its third degree.

- **Lydian:** contains the notes of the major scale starting from its fourth degree.

- **Mixolydian:** contains the notes of the major scale starting from its fifth degree.

- **Aeolian:** contains the notes of the major scale starting from its sixth degree.

- **Locrian:** contains the notes of the major scale starting from its seventh degree.

Even though the major scale and its modal scales use the same notes, because they have different keynotes they do not have the same tonality.

For example, while the major scale has a major third interval from the root to the third note and a major seventh interval from the root to the seventh note, in contrast, the Dorian modal scale has a **flattened third interval** from the root to the third note and a **flattened seventh interval** from the root to the seventh note, making it a type of minor scale.

FREE ACCESS on iPhone & Android etc, using any free QR code app

Scan to **HEAR** the C major chord, and access the full library of scales and chords on flametreemusic.com

START
HERE

BASICS

A

A#/Bb

B

C

C#/Db

D

D#/Eb

E

F

F#/Gb

G

G#/Ab

Modal scales can be used for improvising and composing melodies. Two different approaches can be taken with regard to them:

- Advanced players sometimes use modal scales as chord scales (using a different mode over each chord).

- Modes can be treated as key centres in their own right, with a group of chords to accompany each modal scale. For example, the D Dorian modal scale (see below) could be used over a D Dorian minor key centre containing any of the following chords: **Dm**, **Em**, **F**, **G**, **Am**, **C**.

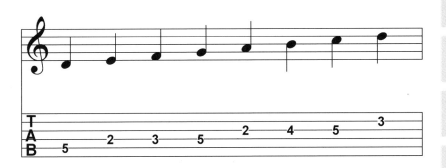

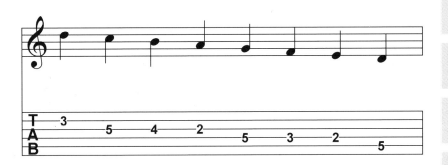

Scan to **HEAR** the C major chord, and access the full library of scales and chords on flametreemusic.com

Types of Scales

The most popular scales used for playing solos can be found in each key from page 44 of this book. In this section, we look at the composition and usage of these more common scales in detail.

This section covers the following scale types:

- Major
- Major Pentatonic
- Lydian
- Natural Minor
- Harmonic Minor
- Melodic Minor

- Dorian
- Minor Pentatonic
- Blues
- Mixolydian
- Wholetone

FREE ACCESS on iPhone & Android etc, using any free QR code app

Scan to **HEAR** the C major chord, and access the full library of scales and chords on flametreemusic.com

Major

By far the most important scale in music is the major scale. All other scales, and even all chords, can be considered as stemming from this scale. It is used as the basis for the majority of popular melodies.

The **third degree** is important in giving a scale its basic flavour; major scales have a major 3rd interval. The scale pattern for the major scale is:

T T S T T T S

This is the most commonly used scale in western music, being the 'Doh, Re, Mi' scale used in *The Sound of Music*. When used in lead playing it gives a **bright and melodic** sound.

As shown on pages 8-9, this pattern gives the C major scale when started on C:

C D E F G A B C

The modes described on pages 12-13 are produced when a major scale begins on a different note in its scale. For example, the notes of C major above could start on the second degree (D), to give the D Dorian scale. As such:

D Dorian = C Major starting and ending on D
E Phrygian = C Major starting and ending on E
F Lydian = C Major starting and ending on F
G Mixolydian = C Major starting and ending on G
A Aeolian (Natural Minor) = C Major starting and ending on A
B Locrian = C Major starting and ending on B

FREE ACCESS on iPhone & Android etc, using any free QR code app

Scan to **HEAR** the C major chord, and access the full library of scales and chords on flametreemusic.com

START
HERE

BASICS

A

A#/B♭

B

C

C#/D♭

D

D#/E♭

E

F

F#/G♭

G

G#/A♭

Major Pentatonic

The term 'pentatonic' means 'five-note'; the pentatonic major scale is a **five-note abbreviation of the standard major scale**, with the fourth and seventh degrees of the major scale omitted. Its scale pattern is:

T T m3 T m3

For example, the notes in the C major scale are C D E F G A B. To convert this into the C pentatonic major scale, omit the notes F (the 4th) and B (the 7th):

C D E G A

The pentatonic major scale has none of the overtly sugary sound often associated with the standard major scale – instead it has a great combination of **brightness with a cutting edge**.

It is a very useful scale for improvising in **major keys**; because it contains fewer notes than the standard major scale there is less chance of any of the notes clashing with the accompanying chords.

Traditionally, pentatonic major scales have been used in country music, but many **rock bands** – from the Rolling Stones and Free to Travis and Supergrass – have used them frequently on their recordings.

Alterations

Sometimes the addition of a minor 3rd note to the pentatonic major scale is used to give a slightly **bluesy edge** to an otherwise major scale. 'New country' and 'country rock' guitar styles favour this sound.

FREE ACCESS on iPhone & Android
etc, using any free QR code app

Scan to **HEAR** the C major chord, and access the full library of scales and chords on flametreemusic.com

Lydian

As explained, the major scale gives rise to a set of **modes**. The Lydian modal scale resembles a major scale except for the **raised fourth degree**. It has a **laid-back** sound that is well-suited to **jazz, fusion and soul music**. Its scale pattern is:

T T T S T T S

For example, the notes of the G major scale are G A B C D E F♯ G. The fourth note in the G major scale is C, so the Lydian modal scale that is generated from the G major scale is the C Lydian modal scale – comprising the notes:

C D E F♯ G A B C

You can see that when compared to the 'tonic major' (the major scale with the same starting note) the only difference is the inclusion of the ♯4 note.

Other Types of Lydian Modal Scales

Lydian Augmented: This is a modal version of the melodic minor and is essentially a Lydian with a raised, or augmented, fifth. Like all scales with an altered fifth it is **restless** and used in **modern jazz**. Its scale pattern is:

T T T T S T S

Lydian Dominant: This is a mode of the melodic minor and has the sharp fourth of a lydian and the flat seventh of a mixolydian. Used mainly in **jazz**. Its scale pattern is:

T T T S T S T

Scan to **HEAR** the C major chord, and access the full library of scales and chords on flametreemusic.com

Natural Minor

This takes a major scale and starts on its **sixth degree**. Significant notes are the flat six and seventh, and the scale pattern is:

T S T T S T T

Using C as a starting note, this produces the C natural minor scale:

C D E♭ F G A♭ B♭ C

T   T   T   T   S   T   T

As this scale contains the same notes as E♭ major (starting on its sixth degree), C minor is the **relative minor** of E♭ major.

Also known as the Aeolian Mode, the natural minor scale is widely used in **rock- and blues-based** music. The scale has a **soulful, yet melodic sound**. Carlos Santana and Gary Moore are two of its best-known exponents.

FREE ACCESS on iPhone & Android etc, using any free QR code app

Scan to **HEAR** the C major chord, and access the full library of scales and chords on flametreemusic.com

Harmonic Minor

START
HERE

BASICS

A

A#/Bb

B

C

C#/Db

D

D#/Eb

E

F

F#/Gb

G

G#/Ab

This is identical to the natural minor except for the **seventh degree**, which is a semitone higher to make a **major dominant chord** possible, essential for most progressions in minor keys.

The harmonic minor scale pattern is:

T S T T S a2 S

Using C as a starting note, applying this pattern will produce the C harmonic minor scale:

C D E♭ F G A♭ B C
T S T T S a2 S

As can be seen, the interval spelling is 1 2 ♭3 4 5 ♭6 7 8. The large interval between the sixth and seventh degrees of the scale gives it its **distinctive**, **exotic** sound.

Ritchie Blackmore was one of the first rock guitarists to exploit the melodic potential of this scale. **Yngwie Malmsteen** also made ample use of harmonic minor scales on his album *Rising Force*.

FREE ACCESS on iPhone & Android etc, using any free QR code app

Scan to **HEAR** the C major chord, and access the full library of scales and chords on flametreemusic.com

START
HERE

BASICS

A

A#/B♭

B

C

C#/D♭

D

D#/E♭

E

F

F#/G♭

G

G#/A♭

Melodic Minor

This is traditionally played with major sixth and seventh on the way up and lowered sixth and seventh on the way down. Its ascending pattern is:

T S T T T T S

The C melodic minor scale ascending is as such:

C D E♭ F G A B C
T S T T T T S

The interval spelling is 1 2 ♭3 4 5 6 7 8 ascending and 1 2 ♭3 4 5 ♭6 ♭7 8 descending. When played descending it has the same notes as the natural minor scale.

Improvising players often abandon the descending version and choose to use exclusively the ascending form, which is consequently more specifically called the **Jazz Melodic Minor**.

In comparison to the natural minor scale, the raised sixth and seventh degrees when ascending give the scale a much **brighter tonality**, making it especially suited to some forms of Jazz music.

FREE ACCESS on iPhone & Android etc, using any free QR code app

Scan to **HEAR** the C major chord, and access the full library of scales and chords on flametreemusic.com

Dorian

This is another important modal scale, also heard in jazz but in many folk songs too. Notice that it has a major sixth but a minor seventh. Its pattern is:

T S T T T S T

As discussed, taking the notes of the major scale starting from its second degree creates the Dorian modal scale. As such, the C Dorian scale contains the same notes as the B♭ major scale, but starting from its second degree:

C D E♭ F G A B♭ C
T S T T T S T

Even though the B♭ major scale and the C Dorian mode derived from it contain the same notes, they have a **very different sound** and character.

For example, the major scale has a major third interval from the first to the third note, and a major seventh interval from the first to the seventh note. In contrast, the Dorian modal scale contains **minor third and minor seventh intervals** – making it a type of 'minor' scale.

Compared to the natural minor scale, the Dorian modal scale has a brighter, **less melancholic**, sound and is often used in funk, soul and jazz styles.

FREE ACCESS on iPhone & Android etc, using any free QR code app

Scan to **HEAR** the C major chord, and access the full library of scales and chords on flametreemusic.com

START
HERE

BASICS

A

A#/Bb

B

C

C#/Db

D

D#/Eb

E

F

F#/Gb

G

G#/Ab

Minor Pentatonic

This is another variant, which could be thought of as a **simplified minor scale** with gaps. Like the major pentatonic, it is often found in folk-melodies but also a favourite with rock guitarists. Its scale pattern is:

m3 T T m3 T

With a starting note of C, this pattern produces the C minor pentatonic scale:

C E♭ F G B♭ C
m3　　T　　T　　m3　　T

The interval spelling is 1 ♭3 4 5 ♭7 8.

It is the **rock-edged** pentatonic minor scale that is by far the most widely used scale in lead-guitar playing. As a pentatonic scale, it offers a quick and simple way of achieving a distinct sound.

It is a **popular** scale for improvising in minor keys because it contains fewer notes than the natural minor scale – this makes the scale **easy to use** and means that there is little chance of any of the notes clashing with the accompanying chords.

FREE ACCESS on iPhone & Android
etc, using any free QR code app

Scan to **HEAR** the C major chord, and access the full library of scales and chords on flametreemusic.com

Blues

This is created by adding one **chromatic note** (a raised fourth or a flattened fifth) to the minor pentatonic scale. It is this note that gives the scale its **distinctive blues flavour**. Its scale pattern is:

m3 T S S m3 T

So the C blues scale contains the following notes:

C E♭ F G♭ G B♭ C
m3   T   S   S   m3   T

All blues lead-guitar playing uses the blues scale as its foundation. It's a minor scale, but it is often used over **major chord progressions**. The blues scale can also be played over a **dominant seventh chord**.

START HERE

BASICS

A

A♯/B♭

B

C

C♯/D♭

D

D♯/E♭

E

F

F♯/G♭

G

G♯/A♭

START
HERE

BASICS

A

A#/B♭

B

C

C#/D♭

D

D#/E♭

E

F

F#/G♭

G

G#/A♭

Mixolydian

This is the most obvious example of a **dominant** type scale, being simply a major scale starting on its fifth degree. You can also think of it as a major scale with a flattened seventh. Used in blues, rock, jazz and folk music, its pattern is:

T T S T T S T

Applying this to the starting note of C, we get the C Mixolydian scale:

C D E F G A B♭ C
T T S T T S T

The C Mixolydian scale contains the same notes as the F major scale, but starting from its **fifth degree**.

The interval spelling of the Mixolydian scale is 1 2 3 4 5 6 ♭7 8.

The essential characteristics of a dominant-type scale are the major third and minor (lowered) seventh. When compared to the 'tonic major' (the major scale with the same starting note), the only difference is the inclusion of the **flat7** note in the Mixolydian modal scale. This gives the scale a **bluesy, yet melodic**, sound.

FREE ACCESS on iPhone & Android etc, using any free QR code app

Scan to **HEAR** the C major chord, and access the full library of scales and chords on flametreemusic.com

Wholetone

The wholetone scale is constructed using only **whole steps**. Between any note and its octave there are six whole steps, therefore the wholetone scale contains six different notes. Its scale pattern is simply:

T T T T T T

So the C wholetone scale is as follows:

C D E F♯ G♯ A♯ C

T T T T T T

The interval spelling is 1 2 3 ♯4 ♯5 ♭7 8.

Wholetone scales are rarely used as key scales, but instead tend to be used for improvising over **dominant altered chords** (such as 7♯5). It's a fairly unusual scale: with the notes equally spaced in pitch, no one tone stands out, giving the scale a curiously indistinct, **dreamlike** quality.

This scale defies much transposition: if you took out every alternate note of a chromatic scale it would make one of the wholetone scales. With a little modification it can also give rise to a further set of modes.

Musical Styles

The following pages introduce some of the main scale soloing techniques that are used for Jazz, Blues and Rock music styles.

Jazz soloing, for example, involves a fair degree of improvisation, and to do this you will need to know a variety of scales and understand which chords they complement. **Listening** to some of your favourite artists can give you an idea of their soloing techniques too. For any type of soloing though, the best way to become skilled in scale use is through **practice**, listening all the while to the sounds you're making. If something sounds intriguing, take the time to play around with it!

Jamming regularly with other musicians can also help make you more comfortable with playing over different chord progressions.

FREE ACCESS on iPhone & Android etc, using any free QR code app

Scan to **HEAR** the C major chord, and access the full library of scales and chords on flametreemusic.com

START HERE

BASICS

A

A♯/B♭

B

C

C♯/D♭

D

D♯/E♭

E

F

F♯/G♭

G

G♯/A♭

Jazz

START
HERE

BASICS

A

A#/Bb

B

C

C#/Db

D

D#/Eb

E

F

F#/Gb

G

G#/Ab

In Jazz soloing, some of the most frequently used chords are the **minor 7**,
dominant 7 and major 7 chords and extensions. There are a number
of appropriate scales to complement these when soloing. All the major scale
modes could be used, but the most important ones in this context are:

- **Dorian**
- **Mixolydian**
- **Ionian (major scale in its tonic position)**

Most jazz tunes also feature **key changes**, so the big challenge in jazz
improvisation is to play over these changes without interrupting the melodic
flow of a solo.

Improvisation within a set piece is best approached by starting with the **basic
melody** of a tune and playing around with **variations** of it. Start with simple
progressions that allow you to improvise with one or two scales, and then
work at jamming over key changes.

For more of a challenge, you can also try '**free improvisation**' – improvising
with others on the spot without any obvious chord progressions or grooves.

Other scales featured in jazz improvisation include:

- **Melodic and harmonic minor scales**
- **Wholetone scale**
- **Diminished scale**
- **Chromatic scale**

The chromatic scale is often used as it contains notes outside the key scale,
which can be used to create **extra tension** in a melody or solo. Chromatic
notes are usually played briefly in phrases that resolve on to key notes,
although they can also be **sustained** to create more tension in the music.

FREE ACCESS on iPhone & Android etc,
using any free QR code app

Scan to **HEAR** the C major chord, and
access the full library of scales and
chords on flametreemusic.com

Blues

Blues is based around the **blues scale**, which is a pentatonic minor scale with an added **flat fifth** note (the 'blue' note). Some examples of great blues guitar soloists include:

- Buddy Guy
- B.B. King
- Robert Johnson
- Muddy Waters

- Stevie Ray Vaughan
- T-Bone Walker
- Eric Clapton
- Elmore James

Blues music is usually played in the keys of **A, D, E and G** as they are all easy keys to play on the guitar. The style has an odd harmonic structure, as the blues scale is usually played or sung over chords that are all **dominant sevenths** (e.g. A7, D7 and E7 in the key of A) or chords derived from them.

The example below is in the style of **John Lee Hooker**, and uses the A minor pentatonic scale as its basis: the first bar involves a quaver run down part of the scale (A, G, E and D). The addition of an E♭ would transform it to a blues scale.

FREE ACCESS on iPhone & Android
etc, using any free QR code app

Scan to **HEAR** the C major chord, and
access the full library of scales and
chords on flametreemusic.com

28

Rock

In all forms of rock music, the **pentatonic minor scale** is the most commonly used scale for lead-guitar playing. Rock solos also often feature the **blues** scale. The **major scale** and the **Mixolydian** mode will add greater depth to your upbeat solos, and the **Aeolian** mode (the natural minor scale) will come in handy for those haunting rock ballads.

Different rock players have very distinctive playing styles. There's an exhaustive list, but just a small selection of notable rock players include:

- Ritchie Blackmore
- Yngwie Malmsteen
- Randy Rhoads
- Eric Johnson
- Uli Jon Roth
- Jimi Hendrix
- David Gilmour
- Jimmy Page
- Pete Townshend
- Eddie Van Halen
- Jeff Beck
- Kirk Hammett
- John Petrucci
- Tony Iommi
- Slash

Below is an example of early rock, in the style of **Jeff Beck** during his Yardbirds era. It uses the D minor pentatonic scale, with the scale played in its full ascending form: D F G A C D.

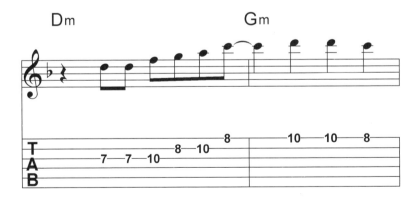

FREE ACCESS on iPhone & Android etc, using any free QR code app

Scan to **HEAR** the C major chord, and access the full library of scales and chords on flametreemusic.com

Other Types of Scales

The scale types listed in the previous pages are given full treatment in the scales section: shown in each key, ascending and descending, in standard and TAB notation.

There are a number of other scales in existence though, which, while less frequently found in popular music, are nevertheless useful to know about, especially if you want to add an especially different flavour to your music. These extra scales are briefly explored in this section, so if you want to use them you can apply the given patterns to any key. You can also head to **flametreemusic.com** for a complete list of scales, common and less common, to see and hear at your leisure.

This section covers the following types of scales:

- Chromatic
- Phrygian
- Phrygian Dominant
- Locrian
- Half Diminished
- Diminished Wholetone/Super Locrian/Altered
- Diminished Wholetone/Octatonic
- Neapolitan
- Bebop
- Byzantine/Arabic/Double Harmonic Major

START HERE

BASICS

A

A#/Bb

B

C

C#/Db

D

D#/Eb

E

F

F#/Gb

G

G#/Ab

START
HERE

BASICS

A

A#/B♭

B

C

C#/D♭

D

D#/E♭

E

F

F#/G♭

G

G#/A♭

FREE ACCESS on iPhone & Android etc, using any free QR code app

Scan to **HEAR** the C major chord, and access the full library of scales and chords on flametreemusic.com

Chromatic

This scale contains every half step between the starting note and the octave.

It is the only 12-note scale in music and does not relate to any particular key. Instead, when improvising, notes from the chromatic scale can be **added** to introduce notes that are not in the key of the backing. Including these 'outside' notes as chromatic passing notes within a lead-guitar solo can help provide moments of **harmonic tension**.

The chromatic scale can be used with **any chord**. As it contains all twelve semitones it can't be transposed or turned into a mode without stubbornly remaining itself.

FREE ACCESS on iPhone & Android etc, using any free QR code app

Scan to **HEAR** the C major chord, and access the full library of scales and chords on flametreemusic.com

Sidebar navigation:
START HERE
BASICS
A
A♯/B♭
B
C
C♯/D♭
D
D♯/E♭
E
F
F♯/G♭
G
G♯/A♭

Phrygian

This is another scale sometimes heard in jazz or folk music. It's identical to the Aeolian/natural minor except for its lowered second step. Its scale pattern is:

S T T T S T T

For example, the C Phrygian scale contains the following notes:

C D♭ E♭ F G A♭ B♭ C

Phrygian Dominant

Also known as the **Spanish Gypsy Scale**, this scale starts on the fifth degree of the harmonic minor scale. Its features are the lowered second and seventh notes, and it works well over a **dominant chord with a flattened ninth**. It is commonly used in flamenco and heavy metal music. Its scale pattern is:

S a2 S T S T T

For example, the C Phrygian Dominant scale contains the following notes:

C D♭ E F G A♭ B♭ C

Scan to **HEAR** the C major chord, and access the full library of scales and chords on flametreemusic.com

START HERE

BASICS

A

A♯/B♭

B

C

C♯/D♭

D

D♯/E♭

E

F

F♯/G♭

G

G♯/A♭

Locrian

This takes the notes of the Phrygian and lowers its fifth step, which gives an **unstable brooding qualit**y to any music using it. Its scale pattern is:

S T T S T T T

The C Locrian scale, therefore, is:

C D♭ E♭ F G♭ A♭ B♭ C

C is the seventh degree of D♭ major, so the C Locrian scale contains the same notes as the D♭ major scale, but starting on C. Because of the change in tonal centre though, the character of the scale is different.

Half Diminished

If we raise the second degree of the Locrian we create this scale, which is also a mode of the melodic minor. Its scale pattern is:

T S T S T T T

The C half diminished scale, therefore, is:

C D E♭ F G♭ A♭ B♭ C

START
HERE

BASICS

A

A♯/B♭

B

C

C♯/D♭

D

D♯/E♭

E

F

F♯/G♭

G

G♯/A♭

Diminished Wholetone/Super Locrian/Altered

This is widely used in jazz and fusion to create a sense of **musical tension** and colour when improvising over **dominant seventh chords**. Its scale pattern is:

S T S T T T T

With a starting note of C, this produces:

C D♭ E♭ F♭ G♭ A♭ B♭ C

Although the third is minor, usually the lowered fourth (identical to a major third) is used to make the essential notes for a dominant chord available: here, the C, F♭ and B♭.

Diminished/Octatonic

This is created by adding the two altered ninths from the scale above to the Lydian Dominant. It has nine different notes and can only be transposed a couple of times before it starts to repeat the same notes. Also used mainly in jazz, its scale pattern is:

S T S T S T S T

With a starting note of C, this produces:

C D♭ E♭ E♮ F♯ G A B♭ C

These are generally used to improvise over **diminished seventh chords**. In C, this chord is formed from the notes C, E♭, F♯ and B♭.

Neapolitan

This a wholetone scale that starts and finishes with a semitone; it is also a melodic minor with a flattened second. Used, like its modes opposite, mainly in jazz and experimental music. Its scale pattern is:

S T T T T S

Types of Neapolitan Scale
The six scales on the page opposite are modes of the Neapolitan scale, and are used in experimental and jazz music.

FREE ACCESS on iPhone & Android etc, using any free QR code app

Scan to **HEAR** the C major chord, and access the full library of scales and chords on flametreemusic.com

36

START
HERE

BASICS

A

A#/Bb

B

C

C#/Db

D

D#/Eb

E

F

F#/Gb

G

G#/Ab

- **Leading Wholetone**: this is the second mode of the Neapolitan, as the name suggests, and is a wholetone with the extra semitone at the top. Its scale pattern is:

T T T T T S S

- **Lydian Augmented Dominant**: the third mode of the Neapolitan scale is a wholetone scale with a major sixth. Its scale pattern is:

T T T T S S T

- **Lydian Dominant ♭6**: this is the fourth mode of the Neapolitan scale and is another wholetone with a perfect fifth available. Its scale pattern is:

T T T S S T T

- **Major Locrian/Arabian**: the fifth mode of the Neapolitan scale, this is a Mixolydian with flat five and six. Its scale pattern is:

T T S S T T T

- **Semi-Locrian ♭4**: this is the sixth mode of the Neapolitan scale, and is a wholetone scale with an added minor third. Its scale pattern is:

T S S T T T T

- **Super Locrian ♭♭3**: this is the seventh and final mode of the Neapolitan. It is more simply thought of as another wholetone with a semitone between the first and second degrees. Its scale pattern is:

S S T T T T T

FREE ACCESS on iPhone & Android etc, using any free QR code app

Scan to **HEAR** the C major chord, and access the full library of scales and chords on flametreemusic.com

Bebop

START HERE

BASICS

A

A#/Bb

B

C

C#/Db

D

D#/Eb

E

F

F#/Gb

G

G#/Ab

There is also a set of so-called Bebop scales, which are simply more familiar scales with an **additional chromatic note**. Bebop scales are frequently used in jazz improvisation. Really any scale can be embellished with a chromatic passing note, but here are a few examples.

- **Bebop Dominant**: this is a Mixolydian with a chromatic major seventh; use as a Mixolydian. Its scale pattern is:

T T S T T S S S

- **Bebop Major**: this has the chromatic passing note between the fifth and sixth degrees. Its scale pattern is:

T T S T T S S T S

- **Bebop Dorian**: this is identical to the regular Dorian with a chromatic major third between the third and fourth steps. Its scale pattern is:

T S S T T S T

In addition, you can always place chromatic notes in other locations (such as between fourth and fifth degrees like a blues scale) and also try turning the bebop scales into modes.

Byzantine/Arabic/Double Harmonic Major

This scale has two augmented seconds. It is an exotic-sounding scale, and is sometimes used in heavy metal or flamenco music.

The **fourth mode** of the Byzantine scale is known as the **Hungarian Minor** scale. Its scale pattern is:

T   S   a2   S   S   a2   S

FREE ACCESS on iPhone & Android etc, using any free QR code app

Scan to **HEAR** the C major chord, and access the full library of scales and chords on flametreemusic.com

Constructing Solos

START
HERE

BASICS

A

A#/Bb

B

C

C#/Db

D

D#/Eb

E

F

F#/Gb

G

G#/Ab

Scales are really suitable for soloing over a **chord sequence**. Once you've selected a scale to use, this will set the range of notes that will fit with the **backing chords**. When starting out, it can be helpful to **spell out** the chords to see which notes they have in common, before choosing relevant scales.

However, you don't need to play all the notes of the scale, or play them in any set order. You should always aim to make your solo sound **fresh and inventive**, rather than scale-like.

Phrasing

Once you've spent hours practising a scale it's all too easy to keep playing it in a continuous way when soloing. Here are some ways to break this habit:

- Leave spaces between notes so that you start to create short phrases
- Use notes of different lengths within the phrases
- Vary the direction in which you play

This rhythmic variety will add interest and shape to your phrases.

To start with, experiment with the C major scale; instead of playing it in strict time, leave some gaps, and balance some longer, **sustained** notes with some very quick **short** notes. There's also no need to play up the whole range of the scale before you play some descending notes – adopt a melodic approach in which your improvisation can **weave** up and down the scale.

FREE ACCESS on iPhone & Android etc, using any free QR code app

Scan to **HEAR** the C major chord, and access the full library of scales and chords on flametreemusic.com

Using Intervals

One thing that always makes a solo sound too scale-like is using notes that are **adjacent** to each other in a scale. This type of playing gives the game away to the listener – they can hear, almost instantly, that the improvisation is derived from a scale. Using **interval gaps** when playing a scale is a perfect way to break away from this scalic sound.

Repetition

By repeating short series of notes you will begin to establish phrases that will give your solo a sense of **structure**. By repeating these phrases, or **variations** on them, you will give the listener something recognizable to latch on to, instead of a seemingly random series of notes with no direction.

Extra Techniques

String bends, vibrato, slides or slurs will all help give your solo an individual **character** and will turn it from a melody into a true guitar solo.

Listen carefully to what is being played on other instruments and your own, trying to make your solo **relate** to the overall musical style of the song.

Scales in Action

These two pages look at some scales in use during guitar solos and riffs. We have seen that the **minor pentatonic** and the **natural minor** scales are good choices for use in rock solos. Above is an example in the style of **Robby Krieger** (of The Doors), which uses the E minor pentatonic scale (see page 128) to complement an Em chord. Below, a riff in the style of Metallica's **Kirk Hammett** shows the E natural minor scale (see page 124). Instead of just being based on a pentatonic scale, the additional notes of F# and C gives it its **Aeolian** tonality. It follows a simple but effective pattern of **fast three-note runs** down the scale.

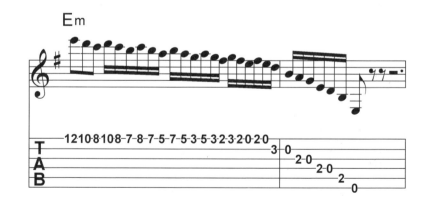

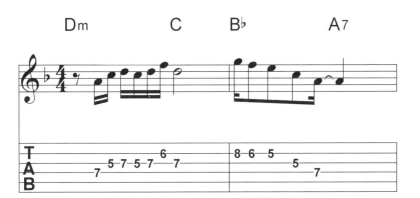

Often, guitarists don't stick to one scale but play around with a few to acheive the desired effect. Above, music in the style of an **Eric Clapton** segment is in D minor, and seems able to straddle both the natural minor and minor pentatonic scales of this key. Below we have something more different: in the style of **Yngwie Malmsteen**, who favours the **Phrygian** mode (see page 33) in his solos. The speedy four-note sequences in this example appear to be based on the E Phrygian scale.

Remember, though, that the best way to become adept at choosing the right scales to solo with is to practise, listening all the while to the effect produced by the various scale types.

FREE ACCESS on iPhone & Android etc, using any free QR code app

Scan to **HEAR** the C major chord, and access the full library of scales and chords on flametreemusic.com

A Major

This scale works well with:
A, Amaj7, D, E, Bm and F♯m

Scale Notes	Up	A B C♯ D E F♯ G♯ A
	Down	A G♯ F♯ E D C♯ B A

FREE ACCESS on iPhone & Android etc. using any free QR code app

Scan to **HEAR** this scale, or go directly to flametreemusic.com

START HERE

BASICS

A

A♯/B♭

B

C

C♯/D♭

D

D♯/E♭

E

F

F♯/G♭

G

G♯/A♭

A Major Pentatonic

This scale works well with: **A, F♯m, Esus2 and Bsus2**
Dickey Betts composed parts of 'Jessica' using this scale, leading into a solo in D major.

START HERE

BASICS

A

A♯/B♭

B

C

C♯/D♭

D

D♯/E♭

E

F

F♯/G♭

G

G♯/A♭

Scale Notes	Up	A B C♯ E F♯ A
	Down	A F♯ E C♯ B A

FREE ACCESS on iPhone & Android etc. using any free QR code app

Scan to **HEAR** this scale, or go directly to flametreemusic.com

A Lydian

This scale works well with:
A, Amaj7, E and B7

Scale Notes	Up	A B C♯ D♯ E F♯ G♯ A
	Down	A G♯ F♯ E D♯ C♯ B A

Scan to **HEAR** this scale, or go directly to flametreemusic.com

A
A♯/B♭
B
C
C♯/D♭
D
D♯/E♭
E
F
F♯/G♭
G
G♯/A♭

START HERE
BASICS

A Natural Minor

This scale works well with: **Am, Am7, Am9 and C**
Gary Moore uses this scale in 'Still Got the Blues'.

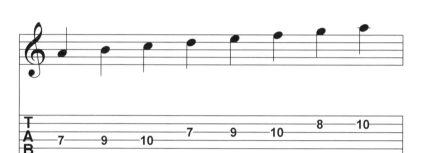

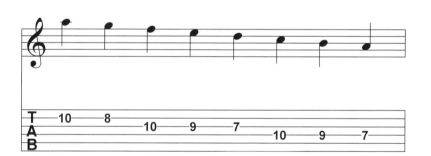

Scale Notes	Up	A B C D E F G A
	Down	A G F E D C B A

Scan to **HEAR** this scale, or go directly to flametreemusic.com

47

A Harmonic Minor

START HERE

BASICS

A

A♯/B♭

B

C

C♯/D♭

D

D♯/E♭

E

F

F♯/G♭

G

G♯/A♭

This scale works well with: **Am, Am-maj7, Dm, E7, Asus2 and Asus4**
Yngwie Malmsteen uses this scale in 'As Above, So Below'.

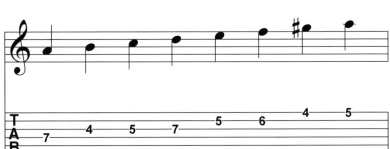

Scale Notes	Up	A B C D E F G♯ A
	Down	A G♯ F E D C B A

FREE ACCESS on iPhone & Android
etc. using any free QR code app

Scan to **HEAR** this scale, or go directly
to flametreemusic.com

A Melodic Minor

This scale works well with:
Am, Am6, Am6/9, Am-maj7, E7 and G♯7

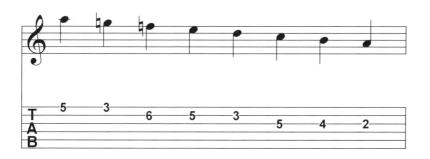

Scale Notes	Up	A B C D E F♯ G♯ A
	Down	A G♮ F♮ E D C B A

START HERE
BASICS
A
A♯/B♭
B
C
C♯/D♭
D
D♯/E♭
E
F
F♯/G♭
G
G♯/A♭

A Dorian

This scale works well with: **A, Am7, Bm7, Asus2 and Asus4**
Carlos Santana solos using this scale in 'Oye Como Va'.

Scale Notes	Up	A B C D E F♯ G A
	Down	A G F♯ E D C B A

FREE ACCESS on iPhone & Android
etc. using any free QR code app

Scan to **HEAR** this scale, or go directly
to flametreemusic.com

A Minor Pentatonic

This scale works well with: **Am**, **A7**, **E7 and C**
Angus Young's solo in 'Highway to Hell' is based around this scale.

START
HERE

BASICS

A

A#/B♭

B

C

C#/D♭

D

D#/E♭

E

F

F#/G♭

G

G#/A♭

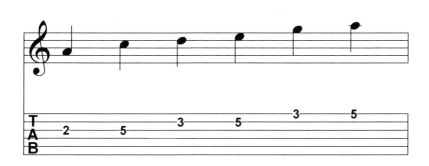

Scale Notes	Up	A C D E G A
	Down	A G E D C A

FREE ACCESS on iPhone & Android
etc. using any free QR code app

Scan to **HEAR** this scale, or go directly
to flametreemusic.com

A Blues

This scale works well with:
A7, D7 and E7

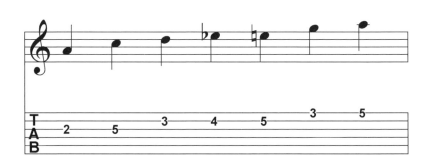

Scale Notes	Up	A C D E♭ E♮ G A
	Down	A G E♮ E♭ D C A

Scan to **HEAR** this scale, or go directly to flametreemusic.com

A Mixolydian

This scale works well with: **A, A7, A9, D, Asus2, A7sus4 and Em**
The solo in 'L.A. Woman' by The Doors uses this scale.

A

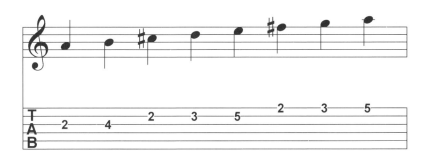

Scale Notes	Up	A B C♯ D E F♯ G A
	Down	A G F♯ E D C♯ B A

FREE ACCESS on iPhone & Android etc. using any free QR code app

Scan to **HEAR** this scale, or go directly to flametreemusic.com

53

A Wholetone

This scale works well with:
A7♯5, A7♯11, A7♭13, A9♯5 and A13♯5

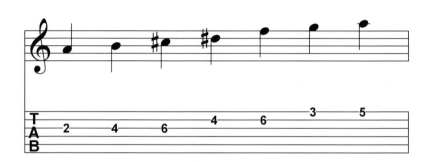

Scale Notes	Up	A B C♯ D♯ F G A
	Down	A G F D♯ C♯ B A

FREE ACCESS on iPhone & Android
etc. using any free QR code app

Scan to **HEAR** this scale, or go directly
to flametreemusic.com

B♭ Major

This scale works well with:
B♭, B♭maj7, E♭, F, Cm, Gm and Dm

START
HERE

BASICS

A

A#/B♭

B

C

C#/D♭

D

D#/E♭

E

F

F#/G♭

G

G#/A♭

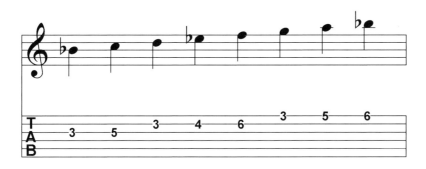

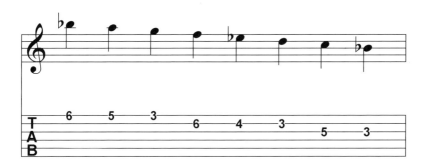

Scale Notes	Up	B♭ C D E♭ F G A B♭
	Down	B♭ A G F E♭ D C B♭

FREE ACCESS on iPhone & Android etc. using any free QR code app

Scan to **HEAR** this scale, or go directly to flametreemusic.com

55

B♭ Major Pentatonic

This scale works well with:
B♭, Gm, Fsus2 and Csus2

Scale Notes	Up	B♭ C D F G B♭
	Down	B♭ G F D C B♭

FREE ACCESS on iPhone & Android
etc. using any free QR code app

Scan to **HEAR** this scale, or go directly
to flametreemusic.com

B♭ Lydian

This scale works well with:
B♭, B♭maj7, F and C7

Scale Notes

Up	B♭ C D E F G A B♭
Down	B♭ A G F E D C B♭

FREE ACCESS on iPhone & Android etc. using any free QR code app

Scan to **HEAR** this scale, or go directly to flametreemusic.com

B♭ Natural Minor

This scale works well with:
B♭m, B♭m7, B♭m9 and D♭

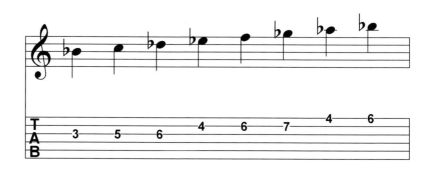

Scale Notes	Up	B♭ C D♭ E♭ F G♭ A♭ B♭
	Down	B♭ A♭ G♭ F E♭ D♭ C B♭

FREE ACCESS on iPhone & Android
etc. using any free QR code app

Scan to **HEAR** this scale, or go directly
to flametreemusic.com

B♭ Harmonic Minor

This scale works well with:
B♭m, B♭m-maj7, E♭m, F7, B♭sus2 and B♭sus4

Scale Notes	Up	B♭ C D♭ E♭ F G♭ A B♭
	Down	B♭ A G♭ F E♭ D♭ C B♭

FREE ACCESS on iPhone & Android etc. using any free QR code app

Scan to **HEAR** this scale, or go directly to flametreemusic.com

B♭ Melodic Minor

This scale works well with:
B♭m, B♭m6, B♭m6/9, B♭m-maj7, F7 and A7

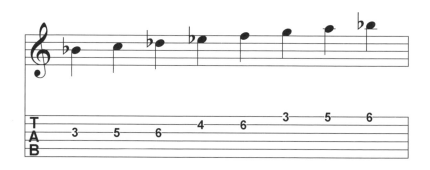

Scale Notes	Up	B♭ C D♭ E♭ F G A B♭
	Down	B♭ A♭ G♭ F E♭ D♭ C B♭

FREE ACCESS on iPhone & Android
etc. using any free QR code app

Scan to **HEAR** this scale, or go directly
to flametreemusic.com

B♭ Dorian

This scale works well with:
B♭m, B♭m7, Cm7, B♭sus2 and B♭sus4

Scale Notes	Up	B♭ C D♭ E♭ F G A♭ B♭
	Down	B♭ A♭ G F E♭ D♭ C B♭

FREE ACCESS on iPhone & Android etc. using any free QR code app

Scan to **HEAR** this scale, or go directly to flametreemusic.com

B♭ Minor Pentatonic

START HERE

BASICS

A

A#/B♭

B

C

C#/D♭

D

D#/E♭

E

F

F#/G♭

G

G#/A♭

This scale works well with:
B♭m, B♭7, F7 and D♭

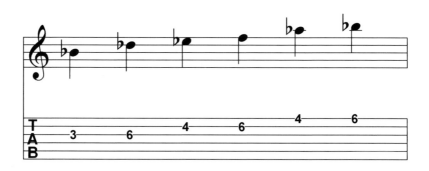

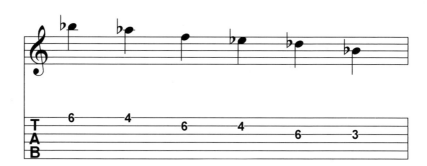

Scale Notes		
	Up	B♭ D♭ E♭ F A♭ B♭
	Down	B♭ A♭ F E♭ D♭ B♭

FREE ACCESS on iPhone & Android etc. using any free QR code app

Scan to **HEAR** this scale, or go directly to flametreemusic.com

B♭ Blues

This scale works well with:
B♭7, E♭7 and F7

Scale Notes	Up	B♭ D♭ E F♭ F♮ A♭ B♭
	Down	B♭ A♭ F♮ F♭ E♭ D♭ B♭

B♭ Mixolydian

This scale works well with:
B♭, B♭7, B♭9, E♭, B♭sus2, B♭7sus4 and Fm

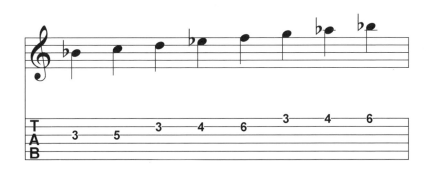

Scale Notes	Up	B♭ C D E♭ F G A♭ B♭
	Down	B♭ A♭ G F E♭ D C B♭

FREE ACCESS on iPhone & Android
etc. using any free QR code app

Scan to **HEAR** this scale, or go directly
to flametreemusic.com

B♭ Wholetone

This scale works well with:
B♭7♯5, B♭7♯11, B♭7♭13, B♭9♯5 and B♭13♯5

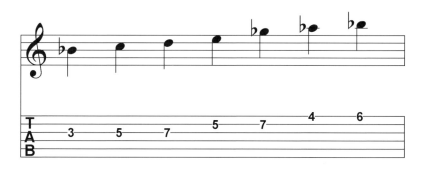

Scale Notes	Up	B♭ C D E G♭ A♭ B♭
	Down	B♭ A♭ G♭ E D C B♭

FREE ACCESS on iPhone & Android etc. using any free QR code app

Scan to **HEAR** this scale, or go directly to flametreemusic.com

B Major

This scale works well with: **B, Bmaj7, E, F♯, C♯m, G♯m and D♯m**
In 'Always With Me, Always With You', Joe Satriani begins his solo
with this scale, leading into B natural minor.

Scale Notes	Up	B C♯ D♯ E F♯ G♯ A♯ B
	Down	B A♯ G♯ F♯ E D♯ C♯ B

FREE ACCESS on iPhone & Android
etc. using any free QR code app

Scan to **HEAR** this scale, or go directly
to flametreemusic.com

B Major Pentatonic

This scale works well with:
B, G♯m, F♯sus2 and C♯sus2

Scale Notes	Up	B C♯ D♯ F♯ G♯ B
	Down	B G♯ F♯ D♯ C♯ B

FREE ACCESS on iPhone & Android etc. using any free QR code app

Scan to **HEAR** this scale, or go directly to flametreemusic.com

START HERE

THE BASICS

A

A♯/B♭

B

C

C♯/D♭

D

D♯/E♭

E

F

F♯/G♭

G

G♯/A♭

B Lydian

This scale works well with:
B, Bmaj7, F# and C#7

Scale Notes	Up	B C# D# E# F# G# A# B
	Down	B A# G# F# E# D# C# B

FREE ACCESS on iPhone & Android
etc. using any free QR code app

Scan to **HEAR** this scale, or go directly
to flametreemusic.com

B Natural Minor

This scale works well with: **Bm, Bm7, Bm9 and D**
Megadeath's Marty Friedman mostly solos with this
scale in 'Tornado of Souls'.

	Up	B C♯ D E F♯ G A B
Scale Notes	Down	B A G F♯ E D C♯ B

B Harmonic Minor

This scale works well with:
Bm, Bm-maj7, Em, F♯7, Bsus2 and Bsus4

Scale Notes	Up	B C♯ D E F♯ G A♯ B
	Down	B A♯ G F♯ E D C♯ B

FREE ACCESS on iPhone & Android
etc. using any free QR code app

Scan to **HEAR** this scale, or go directly
to flametreemusic.com

B Melodic Minor

This scale works well with:
Bm, Bm6, Bm6/9, Bm-maj7, F♯7 and A♯7

Scale Notes	Up	B C♯ D E F♯ G♯ A♯ B
	Down	B A♮ G♮ F♯ E D C♯ B

Scan to **HEAR** this scale, or go directly
to flametreemusic.com

B Dorian

This scale works well with:
Bm, Bm7, C#m7, Bsus2, and Bsus4

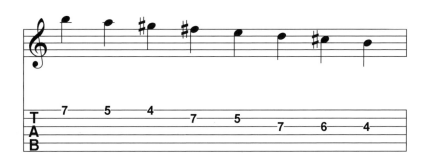

Scale Notes	Up	B C# D E F# G# A B
	Down	B A G# F# E D C# B

FREE ACCESS on iPhone & Android
etc. using any free QR code app

Scan to **HEAR** this scale, or go directly
to flametreemusic.com

B Minor Pentatonic

This scale works well with: **Bm**, **B7**, **F♯7 and D**
With slight modifications, this scale is a close match to the one used to solo with in The Eagles' 'Hotel California'.

Scale Notes	Up	B D E F♯ A B
	Down	B A F♯ E D B

FREE ACCESS on iPhone & Android etc. using any free QR code app

Scan to **HEAR** this scale, or go directly to flametreemusic.com

B Blues

This scale works well with: **B7, E7 and F♯7**
In Pink Floyd's 'Comfortably Numb', David Gilmour mostly solos
with this and B minor pentatonic.

Scale Notes	Up	B D E F♮ F♯ A B
	Down	B A F♯ F♮ E D B

FREE ACCESS on iPhone & Android
etc. using any free QR code app

Scan to **HEAR** this scale, or go directly
to flametreemusic.com

B Mixolydian

This scale works well with: **B**, **B7**, **B9**, **E**, **Bsus2**, **B7sus4 and F#**
Jerry Garcia's solos in The Grateful Dead's 'Sugaree' use this scale.

Scale Notes	Up	B C# D# E F# G# A B
	Down	B A G# F# E D# C# B

Scan to **HEAR** this scale, or go directly
to flametreemusic.com

B Wholetone

This scale works well with:
B7#5, B7#11, B7#11, B7♭13, B9#5, B13#5

Scale Notes	Up	B C# D# F G A B
	Down	B A G F D# C# B

FREE ACCESS on iPhone & Android
etc. using any free QR code app

Scan to **HEAR** this scale, or go directly
to flametreemusic.com

C Major

This scale works well with: **C**, **Cmaj7**, **F**, **G**, **Dm**, **Am and Em**
Led Zeppelin's Jimmy Page uses this scale in 'Fool in the Rain'.

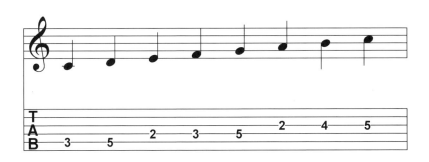

Scale Notes	Up	C D E F G A B C
	Down	C B A G F E D C

FREE ACCESS on iPhone & Android
etc. using any free QR code app

Scan to **HEAR** this scale, or go directly
to flametreemusic.com

77

C Major Pentatonic

This scale works well with: **C, Am, Gsus2 and Dsus2**
Noel Gallagher solos with this scale in 'Don't Look Back in Anger'.

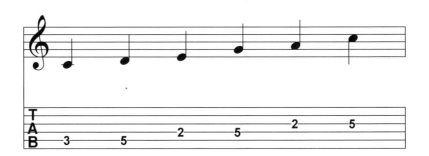

Scale Notes	Up	C D E G A C
	Down	C A G E D C

FREE ACCESS on iPhone & Android
etc. using any free QR code app

Scan to **HEAR** this scale, or go directly
to flametreemusic.com

C Lydian

This scale works well with: **C**, **Cmaj7**, **G** and **D7**
Joe Satriani uses this scale in 'Flying in a Blue Dream'.

Scale Notes	Up	C D E F♯ G A B C
	Down	C B A G F♯ E D C

FREE ACCESS on iPhone & Android
etc. using any free QR code app

Scan to **HEAR** this scale, or go directly
to flametreemusic.com

C Natural Minor

This scale works well with: **Cm, Cm7, Cm9 and E♭**
Marilyn Manson uses this scale to solo in 'Sweet Dreams'.

Scale Notes	Up	C D E♭ F G A♭ B♭ C
	Down	C B♭ A♭ G F E♭ D C

FREE ACCESS on iPhone & Android
etc. using any free QR code app

Scan to **HEAR** this scale, or go directly
to flametreemusic.com

C Harmonic Minor

This scale works well with:
Cm, Cm-maj7, Fm, G7, Csus2 and Csus4

Scale Notes	Up	C D E♭ F G A♭ B C
	Down	C B A♭ G F E♭ D C

FREE ACCESS on iPhone & Android
etc. using any free QR code app

Scan to HEAR this scale, or go directly
to flametreemusic.com

START
HERE

BASICS

A

A♯/B♭

B

C

C♯/D♭

D

D♯/E♭

E

F

F♯/G♭

G

G♯/A♭

C Melodic Minor

This scale works well with:
Cm, Cm6, Cm6/9, Cm-maj7, G7 and B7

Scale Notes	Up	C D E♭ F G A B C
	Down	C B♭ A♭ G F E♭ D C

Scan to **HEAR** this scale, or go directly to flametreemusic.com

C Dorian

This scale works well with:
Cm, Cm7, Dm7, Csus2 and Csus4

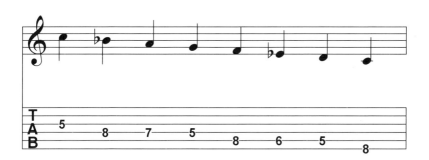

Scale Notes	Up	C D E♭ F G A B♭ C
	Down	C B♭ A G F E♭ D C

Scan to **HEAR** this scale, or go directly to flametreemusic.com

C Minor Pentatonic

This scale works well with:
Cm, C7, G7 and E♭

Scale Notes	Up	C E♭ F G B♭ C
	Down	C B♭ G F E♭ C

FREE ACCESS on iPhone & Android etc. using any free QR code app

Scan to **HEAR** this scale, or go directly to flametreemusic.com

Sidebar navigation: START HERE, BASICS, A, A#/B♭, B, C, C#/D♭, D, D#/E♭, E, F, F#/G♭, G, G#/A♭

C Blues

This scale works well with:
C7, F7 and G7

Scale Notes	Up	C E♭ F G♭ G♮ B♭ C
	Down	C B♭ G♮ G♭ F E♭ C

FREE ACCESS on iPhone & Android etc. using any free QR code app

Scan to **HEAR** this scale, or go directly to flametreemusic.com

C Mixolydian

This scale works well with: **C, C7, C9, F, Csus2, C7sus4 and Gm**
The Beatles' 'Tomorrow Never Knows' has a flavour of this scale.

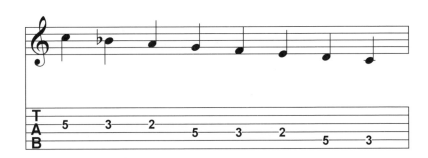

Scale Notes	Up	C D E F G A B♭ C
	Down	C B♭ A G F E D C

FREE ACCESS on iPhone & Android
etc. using any free QR code app

Scan to **HEAR** this scale, or go directly
to flametreemusic.com

C Wholetone

This scale works well with:
C7#5, C7#11, C7♭13, C9#5 and C13#5

Scale Notes	Up	C D E F# G# A# C
	Down	C A# G# F# E D C

FREE ACCESS on iPhone & Android
etc. using any free QR code app

Scan to **HEAR** this scale, or go directly
to flametreemusic.com

D♭ Major

This scale works well with:
D♭, D♭maj7, G♭, A♭, E♭m, B♭m and Fm

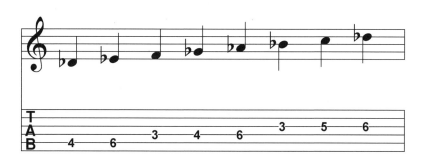

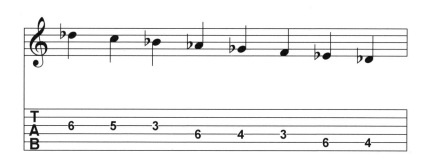

Scale Notes	Up	D♭ E♭ F G♭ A♭ B♭ C D♭
	Down	D♭ C B♭ A♭ G♭ F E♭ D♭

FREE ACCESS on iPhone & Android etc. using any free QR code app

Scan to **HEAR** this scale, or go directly to flametreemusic.com

D♭ Major Pentatonic

This scale works well with:
D♭, B♭m, A♭sus2 and E♭sus4

Scale Notes	Up	D♭ E♭ F A♭ B♭ D♭
	Down	D♭ B♭ A♭ F E♭ D♭

C#/D♭

D♭ Lydian

This scale works well with:
D♭, D♭maj7, A♭ and E♭7

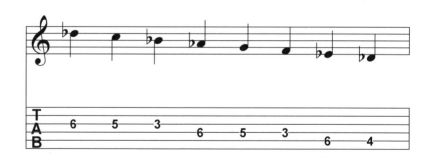

Scale Notes	Up	D♭ E♭ F G A♭ B♭ C D♭
	Down	D♭ C B♭ A♭ G F E♭ D♭

Scan to **HEAR** this scale, or go directly
to flametreemusic.com

90

C♯ Natural Minor

This scale works well with:
C♯m, C♯m7, C♯m9 and E

Scale Notes	Up	C♯ D♯ E F♯ G♯ A B C♯
	Down	C♯ B A G♯ F♯ E D♯ C♯

FREE ACCESS on iPhone & Android
etc. using any free QR code app

Scan to **HEAR** this scale, or go directly
to flametreemusic.com

C# Harmonic Minor

This scale works well with:

C#m, C#m-maj7, F#m, G#7, C#sus2 and C#sus4

Scale Notes	Up	C# D# E F# G# B# C#
	Down	C# B# A G# F# E D# C#

FREE ACCESS on iPhone & Android
etc. using any free QR code app

Scan to **HEAR** this scale, or go directly
to flametreemusic.com

C# Melodic Minor

This scale works well with:
C#m, C#m6, C#m6/9, C#m-maj7, G#7 and B#7

Scale Notes	Up	C# D# E F# G# A# B# C#
	Down	C# B♮ A♮ G# F# E D# C#

Tab numbers (first staff): 4 6 7 4 6 3 5 6

Tab numbers (second staff): 6 4 7 6 4 7 6 4

C# Dorian

This scale works well with:
C#m, C#m7, D#m7, C#sus2 and C#sus4

Scale Notes	Up	C# D# E F# G# A# B C#
	Down	C# B A# G# F# E D# C#

Scan to **HEAR** this scale, or go directly to flametreemusic.com

C# Minor Pentatonic

This scale works well with:
C#m, C#7, G#7 and E

Scale Notes	Up	C# E F# G# B C#
	Down	C# B G# F# E C#

FREE ACCESS on iPhone & Android etc. using any free QR code app

Scan to **HEAR** this scale, or go directly to flametreemusic.com

C# Blues

This scale works well with:
C#7, F#7 and G#7

Scale Notes	Up	C# E F# G♮ G# B C#
	Down	C# B G# G♮ F# E C#

A
A#/B♭
B
C
C#/D♭
D
D#/E♭
E
F
F#/G♭
G
G#/A♭

START HERE

BASICS

C♯ Mixolydian

This scale works well with: **C♯, C♯7, C♯9, F♯, C♯sus2, C♯7sus4 and G♯m**
George Harrison wrote 'Within You Without You' around this scale.

	Scale Notes		
Up	C♯ D♯ E♯ F♯ G♯ A♯ B C♯
Down	C♯ B A♯ G♯ F♯ E♯ D♯ C♯

FREE ACCESS on iPhone & Android etc. using any free QR code app

Scan to **HEAR** this scale, or go directly to flametreemusic.com

D♭ Wholetone

This scale works well with:
D♭7#5, D♭7#11, D♭7♭13, D♭9#5 and D♭13#5

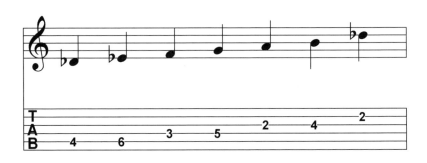

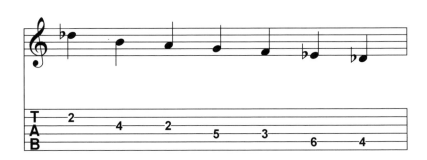

Scale Notes	Up	D♭ E♭ F G A B D♭
	Down	D♭ B A G F E♭ D♭

FREE ACCESS on iPhone & Android etc. using any free QR code app

Scan to **HEAR** this scale, or go directly to flametreemusic.com

D Major

This scale works well with: **D**, **Dmaj7**, **G**, **A**, **Em**, **Bm and F#m**
The first solo in Pink Floyd's 'Comfortably Numb' uses this scale.

Scale Notes	Up	D E F# G A B C# D
	Down	D C# B A G F# E D

START
HERE

BASICS

A

A#/Bb

B

C

C#/Db

D

D#/Eb

E

F

F#/Gb

G

G#/Ab

D Major Pentatonic

This scale works well with: **D, Bm, Gsus2 and Esus2**
The solo in Lynyrd Skynyrd's 'Gimme Three Steps' uses this scale.

Scale Notes	Up	D E F♯ A B D
	Down	D B A F♯ E D

D Lydian

This scale works well with:
D, Dmaj7, A and E7

Scale Notes	Up	D E F# G# A B C# D
	Down	D C# B A G# F# E D

D Natural Minor

This scale works well with:
Dm, Dm7, Dm9 and F

Scale Notes	Up	D E F G A Bb C D
	Down	D C Bb A G F E D

FREE ACCESS on iPhone & Android
etc. using any free QR code app

Scan to **HEAR** this scale, or go directly
to flametreemusic.com

D Harmonic Minor

START HERE

BASICS

A

A#/Bb

B

C

C#/Db

D

D#/Eb

E

F

F#/Gb

G

G#/Ab

This scale works well with:
Dm, Dm-maj7, Gm, A7, Dsus2 and Dsus4

Scale Notes	Up	D E F G A Bb C# D
	Down	D C# Bb A G F E D

FREE ACCESS on iPhone & Android
etc. using any free QR code app

Scan to **HEAR** this scale, or go directly
to flametreemusic.com

D Melodic Minor

This scale works well with: **Dm, Dm6, Dm6/9, Dm-maj7, A7 and C#7**
'Yesterday' by The Beatles uses part of this scale.

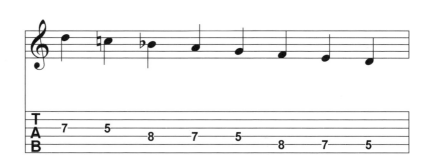

Scale Notes	Up	D E F G A B C# D
	Down	D C# B♭ A G F E D

D Dorian

This scale works well with: **Dm, Dm7, Em7, Dsus2 and Dsus4**
Miles Davis uses this scale in 'So What'.

Scale Notes	Up	D E F G A B C D
	Down	D C B A G F E D

Scan to **HEAR** this scale, or go directly
to flametreemusic.com

D Minor Pentatonic

This scale works well with: **Dm, D7, G7 and F**
The opening of Eric Clapton's 'Layla' uses a variation of this scale.

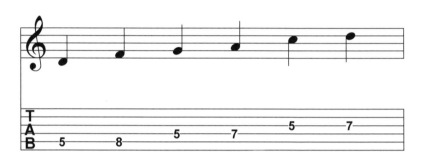

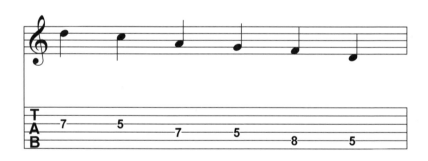

Scale Notes	Up	D F G A C D
	Down	D C A G F A

Scan to **HEAR** this scale, or go directly to flametreemusic.com

D Blues

This scale works well with:
D7, G7 and A7

		Scale Notes	
Scale Notes	Up	D F G A♭ A♮ C D	
	Down	D C A♮ A♭ G F D	

Scan to **HEAR** this scale, or go directly
to flametreemusic.com

START HERE

BASICS

A

A♯/B♭

B

C

C♯/D♭

D

D♯/E♭

E

F

F♯/G♭

G

G♯/A♭

D Mixolydian

This scale works well with: **D, D7, D9, G, Dsus2, D7sus4 and Am**
Slash's intro solo to 'Sweet Child O' Mine' plays around this scale.

Scale Notes	Up	D E F♯ G A B C D
	Down	D C B A G F♯ E D

FREE ACCESS on iPhone & Android
etc. using any free QR code app

Scan to **HEAR** this scale, or go directly
to flametreemusic.com

START HERE

BASICS

A

A♯/B♭

B

C

C♯/D♭

D

D♯/E♭

E

F

F♯/G♭

G

G♯/A♭

D Wholetone

This scale works well with:
D7#5, D7#11, D7♭13, D9#5 and D13#5

Scale Notes	Up	D E F# G# A# C D
	Down	D C A# G# F# E D

E♭ Major

This scale works well with:
E♭, E♭maj7, A♭, B♭, Fm, Cm, and Gm

Scale Notes	Up	E♭ F G A♭ B♭ C D E♭
	Down	E♭ D C B♭ A♭ G F E♭

FREE ACCESS on iPhone & Android etc. using any free QR code app

Scan to **HEAR** this scale, or go directly to flametreemusic.com

E♭ Major Pentatonic

This scale works well with:
E♭, Cm, B♭sus2 and Fsus2

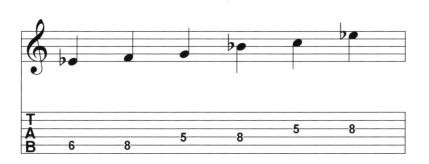

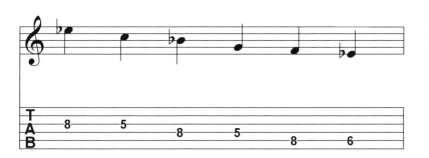

Scale Notes	Up	E♭ F G B♭ C E♭
	Down	E♭ C B♭ G F E♭

Scan to **HEAR** this scale, or go directly to flametreemusic.com

E♭ Lydian

This scale works well with:
E♭, E♭maj7, B♭ and F7

Scale Notes	Up	E♭ F G A B♭ C D E♭
	Down	E♭ D C B♭ A G F E♭

FREE ACCESS on iPhone & Android
etc. using any free QR code app

Scan to **HEAR** this scale, or go directly
to flametreemusic.com

START HERE

BASICS

A

A#/B♭

B

C

C#/D♭

D

D#/E♭

E

F

F#/G♭

G

G#/A♭

E♭ Natural Minor

This scale works well with:
E♭m, E♭m7, E♭m9 and G♭

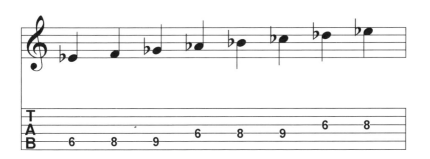

START
HERE

BASICS

A

A♯/B♭

B

C

C♯/D♭

D

D♯/E♭

E

F

F♯/G♭

G

G♯/A♭

Scale Notes	Up	E♭ F G♭ A♭ B♭ C♭ D♭ E♭
	Down	E♭ D♭ C♭ B♭ A♭ G♭ F E♭

FREE ACCESS on iPhone & Android
etc. using any free QR code app

Scan to **HEAR** this scale, or go directly
to flametreemusic.com

E♭ Harmonic Minor

This scale works well with:
E♭m, E♭m-maj7, C♭m, B♭7, E♭sus2 and E♭7sus4

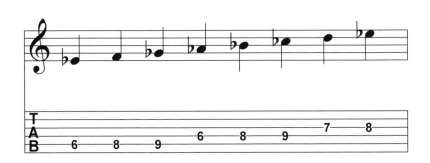

Scale Notes	Up	E♭ F G♭ A♭ B♭ C♭ D E♭
	Down	E♭ D C♭ B♭ A♭ G♭ F E♭

FREE ACCESS on iPhone & Android
etc. using any free QR code app

Scan to **HEAR** this scale, or go directly
to flametreemusic.com

E♭ Melodic Minor

This scale works well with:
E♭m, E♭m6, E♭m6/9, E♭m-maj7, B♭7 and D7

START
HERE

BASICS

A

A♯/B♭

B

C

C♯/D♭

D

D♯/E♭

E

F

F♯/G♭

G

G♯/A♭

Scale Notes	Up	E♭ F G♭ A♭ B♭ C D E♭
	Down	E♭ D♭ C♭ B♭ A♭ G♭ F E♭

FREE ACCESS on iPhone & Android
etc. using any free QR code app

Scan to **HEAR** this scale, or go directly
to flametreemusic.com

E♭ Dorian

This scale works well with:
E♭m, E♭m7, Fm7, E♭sus2 and E♭sus4

Scale Notes	Up	E♭ F G♭ A♭ B♭ C D♭ E♭
	Down	E♭ D♭ C B♭ A♭ G♭ F E♭

FREE ACCESS on iPhone & Android
etc. using any free QR code app

Scan to **HEAR** this scale, or go directly
to flametreemusic.com

START HERE

BASICS

A

A#/B♭

B

C

C#/D♭

D

D#/E♭

E

F

F#/G♭

G

G#/A♭

E♭ Minor Pentatonic

This scale works well with:
E♭m, E♭7, B♭7 and G♭

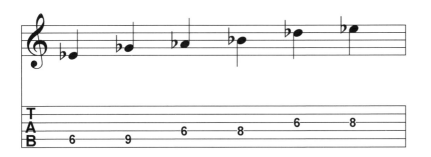

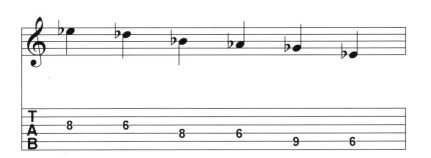

Scale Notes	Up	E♭ G♭ A♭ B♭ D♭ E♭
	Down	E♭ D♭ B♭ A♭ G♭ E♭

START
HERE

BASICS

A

A♯/B♭

B

C

C♯/D♭

D

D♯/E♭

E

F

F♯/G♭

G

G♯/A♭

D♯ Blues

This scale works well with:
D♯7, G♯7 and A♯7

Scale Notes	Up	D♯ F♯ G♯ A♮ A♯ C♯ D♯
	Down	D♯ C♯ A♯ A♮ G♯ F♯ D♯

FREE ACCESS on iPhone & Android etc. using any free QR code app

Scan to **HEAR** this scale, or go directly to flametreemusic.com

E♭ Mixolydian

This scale works well with:
E♭, E♭7, E♭9, A♭, E♭sus2, E♭7sus4 and B♭m

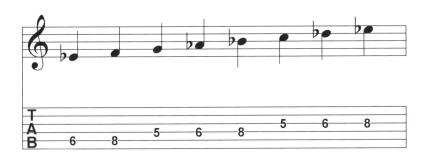

	Up	E♭ F G A♭ B♭ C D♭ E♭
Scale Notes	Down	E♭ D♭ C B♭ A♭ G F E♭

FREE ACCESS on iPhone & Android etc. using any free QR code app

Scan to **HEAR** this scale, or go directly to flametreemusic.com

E♭ Wholetone

This scale works well with:
E♭7#5, E♭7#11, E♭7♭13, E♭9#5 and E♭13#5

Scale Notes	Up	E♭ F G A B D♭ E♭
	Down	E♭ D♭ B A G F E♭

Scan to **HEAR** this scale, or go directly to flametreemusic.com

START HERE

BASICS

A

A#/B♭

B

C

C#/D♭

D

D#/E♭

E

F

F#/G♭

G

G#/A♭

E Major

This scale works well with: **E, Emaj7, A, B, F#m, C#m and G#m**
The solo in The Allman Brothers Band's 'Blue Sky' uses a
Hexatonic version of this scale.

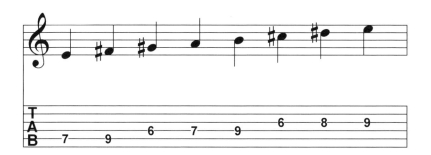

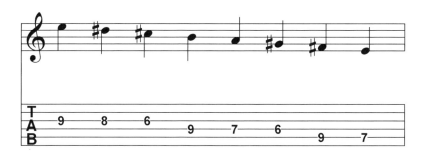

| **Scale Notes** | Up | E F# G# A B C# D# E |
| | Down | E D# C# B A G# F# E |

START
HERE

BASICS

A

A#/Bb

B

C

C#/Db

D

D#/Eb

E

F

F#/Gb

G

G#/Ab

E Major Pentatonic

This scale works well with:
E, C#m, Bsus2 and F#sus2

Scale Notes	Up	E F# G# B C# E
	Down	E C# B G# F# E

FREE ACCESS on iPhone & Android
etc. using any free QR code app

Scan to **HEAR** this scale, or go directly
to flametreemusic.com

E Lydian

This scale works well with:
E, Emaj7, B and F#7

Scale Notes	Up	E F# G# A# B C# D# E
	Down	E D# C# B A# G# F# E

FREE ACCESS on iPhone & Android etc. using any free QR code app

Scan to **HEAR** this scale, or go directly to flametreemusic.com

123

E Natural Minor

This scale works well with:
Em, Em7, Em9 and G

Scale Notes	Up	E F♯ G A B C D E
	Down	E D C B A G F♯ E

FREE ACCESS on iPhone & Android
etc. using any free QR code app

Scan to **HEAR** this scale, or go directly
to flametreemusic.com

E Harmonic Minor

START
HERE

BASICS

A

A#/Bb

B

C

C#/Db

D

D#/Eb

E

F

F#/Gb

G

G#/Ab

This scale works well with: **Em, Em-maj7, Am, B7, Esus2 and Esus4**
Black Sabbath's Tony Iommi made great use of this scale in his early work.

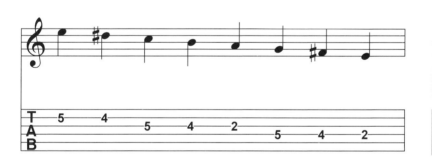

Scale Notes	Up	E F♯ G A B C D♯ E
	Down	E D♯ C B A G F♯ E

FREE ACCESS on iPhone & Android etc. using any free QR code app

Scan to **HEAR** this scale, or go directly to flametreemusic.com

E Melodic Minor

This scale works well with:
Em, Em6, Em6/9, Em-maj7, B7 and D♯7

Scale Notes	Up	E F♯ G A B C♯ D♯ E
	Down	E D♮ C♮ B A G F♯ E

E Dorian

This scale works well with: **Em, Em7, F#m7, Esus2 and Esus4**
Soundgarden's 'Loud Love' uses this scale.

Scale Notes		
	Up	E F# G A B C# D E
	Down	E D C# B A G F# E

E Minor Pentatonic

This scale works well over the chords: **G, Em, E7 and A7**
Jimi Hendrix uses this scale in 'Voodoo Child'.

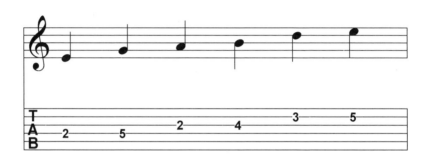

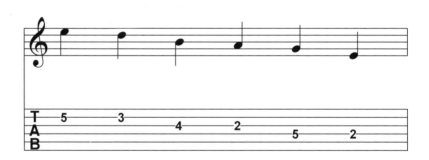

Scale Notes	Up	E G A B D E
	Down	E D B A G E

Scan to **HEAR** this scale, or go directly
to flametreemusic.com

E Blues

This scale works well with:
E7, A7 and B7

Scale Notes	Up	E G A B♭ B♮ D E
	Down	E D B♮ B♭ A G E

E Mixolydian

This scale works well with: **E, E7, E9, A, Esus2, E7sus4 and Bm**
Soloing in The Beatles' 'Day Tripper' uses this scale.

Scale Notes	Up	E F♯ G♯ A B C♯ D E
	Down	E D C♯ B A G♯ F♯ E

FREE ACCESS on iPhone & Android
etc. using any free QR code app

Scan to **HEAR** this scale, or go directly
to flametreemusic.com

E Wholetone

This scale works well with:
E7♯5, E7♯11, E7♭13, E9♯5 and E13♯5

Scale Notes	Up	E F♯ G♯ A♯ C D E
	Down	E D C A♯ G♯ F♯ E

START HERE

BASICS

A

A♯/B♭

B

C

C♯/D♭

D

D♯/E♭

E

F

F♯/G♭

G

G♯/A♭

F Major

This scale works well with: **F**, **Fmaj7**, **B♭**, **C**, **Gm**, **Dm and Am**
Solos use this scale in 'The Joker' by Steve Miller Band.

Scale Notes	Up	F G A B♭ C D E F
	Down	F E D C B♭ A G F

FREE ACCESS on iPhone & Android
etc. using any free QR code app

Scan to **HEAR** this scale, or go directly
to flametreemusic.com

F Major Pentatonic

This scale works well with:
F, Dm, Csus2 and Gsus2

Scale Notes	Up	F G A C D F
	Down	F D C A G F

F Lydian

This scale works well with:
F, Fmaj7, C and G7

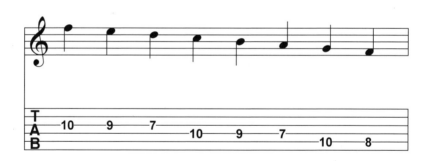

Scale Notes	Up	F G A B C D E F
	Down	F E D C B A G F

FREE ACCESS on iPhone & Android
etc. using any free QR code app

Scan to **HEAR** this scale, or go directly
to flametreemusic.com

F Natural Minor

START HERE

BASICS

This scale works well with: **Fm**, **Fm7**, **Fm9 and A♭**
Kurt Cobain uses this scale to solo in 'Smells like Teen Spirit'

Scale Notes	Up	F G A♭ B♭ C D♭ E♭ F
	Down	F E♭ D♭ C B♭ A♭ G F

FREE ACCESS on iPhone & Android etc. using any free QR code app

Scan to **HEAR** this scale, or go directly to flametreemusic.com

F Harmonic Minor

This scale works well with:
Fm, Fm-maj7, B♭m, C7, Fsus2 and Fsus4

Scale Notes	Up	F G A♭ B♭ C D♭ E F
	Down	F E D♭ C B♭ A♭ G F

Scan to **HEAR** this scale, or go directly to flametreemusic.com

F Melodic Minor

This scale works well with:
Fm, Fm6, Fm6/9, Fm-maj7, C7 and E7

Scale Notes	Up	F G A♭ B♭ C D E F
	Down	F E♭ D♭ C B♭ A♭ G F

FREE ACCESS on iPhone & Android
etc. using any free QR code app

Scan to **HEAR** this scale, or go directly
to flametreemusic.com

137

F Dorian

This scale works well with:
Fm, Fm7, Gm7, Fsus2 and Fsus4

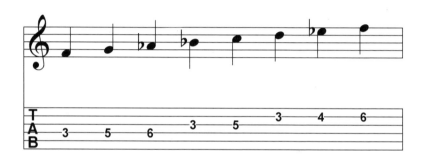

Scale Notes	Up	F G A♭ B♭ C D E♭ F
	Down	F E♭ D C B♭ A♭ G F

FREE ACCESS on iPhone & Android etc. using any free QR code app

Scan to **HEAR** this scale, or go directly to flametreemusic.com

F Minor Pentatonic

This scale works well with:
Fm, F7, C7 and A♭

Scale Notes	Up	F A♭ B♭ C E♭ F
	Down	F E♭ C B♭ A♭ F

FREE ACCESS on iPhone & Android
etc. using any free QR code app

Scan to **HEAR** this scale, or go directly
to flametreemusic.com

F Blues

This scale works well with: **F7, B♭7 and C7**
Ritchie Blackmore's 'Lazy' uses patterns based on this scale.

Scale Notes	Up	F A♭ B♭ C♭ C♮ E♭ F
	Down	F E♭ C♮ C♭ B♭ A♭ F

FREE ACCESS on iPhone & Android
etc. using any free QR code app

Scan to **HEAR** this scale, or go directly
to flametreemusic.com

F Mixolydian

This scale works well with:

F, F7, F9, B♭, Fsus2, F7sus4 and Cm

Scale Notes	Up	F G A B♭ C D E♭ F
	Down	F E♭ D C B♭ A G F

FREE ACCESS on iPhone & Android
etc. using any free QR code app

Scan to **HEAR** this scale, or go directly
to flametreemusic.com

141

F Wholetone

This scale works well with:
F7#5, F7#11, F7♭13, F9#5 and F13#5

Scale Notes	Up	F G A B C# D# F
	Down	F D# C# B A G F

FREE ACCESS on iPhone & Android
etc. using any free QR code app

Scan to **HEAR** this scale, or go directly
to flametreemusic.com

F# Major

This scale works well with:
F#, F#maj7, B, C#, G#m, D#m and A#m

START
HERE

BASICS

A

A#/Bb

B

C

C#/Db

D

D#/Eb

E

F

F#/Gb

G

G#/Ab

Scale Notes		
	Up	F# G# A# B C# D# E# F#
	Down	F# E# D# C# B A# G# F#

FREE ACCESS on iPhone & Android
etc. using any free QR code app

Scan to **HEAR** this scale, or go directly
to flametreemusic.com

F♯ Major Pentatonic

This scale works well with:
F♯, D♯m, C♯sus2 and G♯sus2

Scale Notes	Up	F♯ G♯ A♯ C♯ D♯ F♯
	Down	F♯ D♯ C♯ A♯ G♯ F♯

FREE ACCESS on iPhone & Android etc. using any free QR code app

Scan to **HEAR** this scale, or go directly to flametreemusic.com

START HERE

THE BASICS

A

A♯/B♭

B

C

C♯/D♭

D

D♯/E♭

E

F

F♯/G♭

G

G♯/A♭

G♭ Lydian

This scale works well with:
G♭, G♭maj7, D♭ and A♭7

Scale Notes	Up	G♭ A♭ B♭ C D♭ E♭ F G♭
	Down	G♭ F E♭ D♭ C B♭ A♭ G♭

Scan to **HEAR** this scale, or go directly to flametreemusic.com

START HERE

THE BASICS

A

A♯/B♭

B

C

C♯/D♭

D

D♯/E♭

E

F

F♯/G♭

G

G♯/A♭

F♯ Natural Minor

This scale works well with: **F♯m, F♯m7, F♯m9 and A**
Randy Rhoads uses this scale in Ozzy Osbourne's 'Crazy Train'.

Scale Notes	Up	F♯ G♯ A B C♯ D E F♯
	Down	F♯ E D C♯ B A G♯ F♯

FREE ACCESS on iPhone & Android
etc. using any free QR code app

Scan to **HEAR** this scale, or go directly
to flametreemusic.com

F# Harmonic Minor

This scale works well with:
F#m, F#m-maj7, Bm, C#7, F#sus2 and F#sus4

Scale Notes	Up	F# G# A B C# D E# F#
	Down	F# E# D C# B A G# F#

F♯ Melodic Minor

This scale works well with:
F♯m, F♯m6, F♯m6/9, F♯m-maj7, C♯7 and E♯7

Scale Notes	Up	F♯ G♯ A B C♯ D♯ E♯ F♯
	Down	F♯ E♮ D♮ C♯ B A G♯ F♯

FREE ACCESS on iPhone & Android etc. using any free QR code app

Scan to **HEAR** this scale, or go directly to flametreemusic.com

148

F# Dorian

This scale works well with:
F#m, F#m7, G#m7, F#sus2 and F#sus4

Scale Notes	Up	F# G# A B C# D# E F#
	Down	F# E D# C# B A G# F#

Scan to **HEAR** this scale, or go directly to flametreemusic.com

F# Minor Pentatonic

This scale works well with:
F#m, F#7, C#7 and A

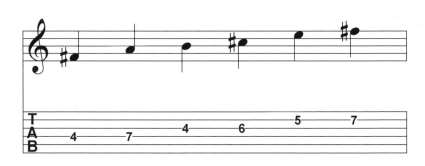

Scale Notes	Up	F# A B C# E F#
	Down	F# E C# B A F#

Scan to **HEAR** this scale, or go directly to flametreemusic.com

START HERE

THE BASICS

A

A#/Bb

B

C

C#/Db

D

D#/Eb

E

F

F#/Gb

G

G#/Ab

F♯ Blues

This scale works well with:
F♯7, B7 and C♯7

Scale Notes	Up	F♯ A B C♮ C♯ E F♯
	Down	F♯ E C♯ C♮ B A F♯

FREE ACCESS on iPhone & Android
etc. using any free QR code app

Scan to **HEAR** this scale, or go directly
to flametreemusic.com

F♯ Mixolydian

This scale works well with:
F♯, F♯7, F♯9, B, F♯sus2, F♯7sus4 and C♯m

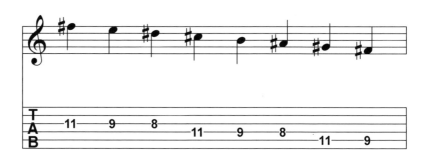

Scale Notes	Up	F♯ G♯ A♯ B C♯ D♯ E F♯
	Down	F♯ E D♯ C♯ B A♯ G♯ F♯

FREE ACCESS on iPhone & Android
etc. using any free QR code app

Scan to **HEAR** this scale, or go directly
to flametreemusic.com

F# Wholetone

This scale works well with:
F#7#5, F#7#11, F#7b13, F#9#5 and F#13#5

Scale Notes	Up	F# G# A# C D E F#
	Down	F# E D C A# G# F#

Scan to **HEAR** this scale, or go directly
to flametreemusic.com

G Major

This scale works well with: **G**, **Gmaj7**, **C**, **D**, **Am**, **Em** and **Bm**
Van Morrison uses this scale for the riff in 'Brown Eyed Girl'.

Scale Notes	**Up**	G A B C D E F♯ G
	Down	G F♯ E D C B A G

Scan to **HEAR** this scale, or go directly
to flametreemusic.com

G Major Pentatonic

This scale works well with:
G, Em, Dsus2 and Asus2

Scale Notes	**Up**	G A B D E G
	Down	G E D B A G

Scan to **HEAR** this scale, or go directly to flametreemusic.com

A

A♯/B♭

B

C

C♯/D♭

D

D♯/E♭

E

F

F♯/G♭

G

G♯/A♭

START HERE

BASICS

G Lydian

This scale works well with:
G, Gmaj7, D and A7

Scale Notes	Up	G A B C♯ D E F♯ G
	Down	G F♯ E D C♯ B A G

Scan to **HEAR** this scale, or go directly to flametreemusic.com

G Natural Minor

START HERE

BASICS

A

A#/B♭

B

C

C#/D♭

D

D#/E♭

E

F

F#/G♭

G

G#/A♭

This scale works well with:
Gm, Gm7, Gm9 and B♭

Scale Notes	Up	G A B♭ C D E♭ F G
	Down	G F E♭ D C B♭ A G

FREE ACCESS on iPhone & Android
etc. using any free QR code app

Scan to **HEAR** this scale, or go directly
to flametreemusic.com

G Harmonic Minor

This scale works well with:
Gm, Gm-maj7, Cm, D7, Gsus2 and Gsus4

Scale Notes	Up	G A B♭ C D E♭ F♯ G
	Down	G F♯ E♭ D C B♭ A G

FREE ACCESS on iPhone & Android
etc. using any free QR code app

Scan to **HEAR** this scale, or go directly
to flametreemusic.com

G Melodic Minor

This scale works well with:

Gm, Gm6, Gm6/9, Gm-maj7, D7 and F♯7

Scale Notes	Up	G A B♭ C D E F♯ G
	Down	G F♮ E♭ D C B♭ A G

Scan to **HEAR** this scale, or go directly to flametreemusic.com

G Dorian

This scale works well with: **Gm, Gm7, Am7, Gsus2 and Gsus4**
Carlos Santana's solo in 'Evil Ways' makes use of this scale.

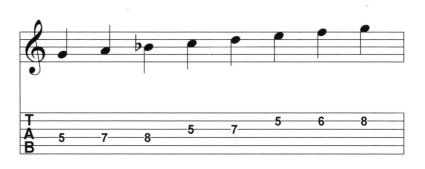

Scale Notes	Up	G A B♭ C D E F G
	Down	G F E D C B♭ A G

A
A♯/B♭
B
C
C♯/D♭
D
D♯/E♭
E
F
F♯/G♭
G
G♯/A♭

START HERE

BASICS

G Minor Pentatonic

This scale works well with:
Gm, G7, D7 and B♭

Scale Notes	Up	G B♭ C D F G
	Down	G F D C B♭ G

Scan to **HEAR** this scale, or go directly to flametreemusic.com

START HERE

BASICS

A

A#/B♭

B

C

C#/D♭

D

D#/E♭

E

F

F#/G♭

G

G#/A♭

G Blues

This scale works well over the chords:
G7, C7 and D7

Scale Notes	Up	G B♭ C D♭ D♮ F G
	Down	G F D♮ D♭ C B♭ G

FREE ACCESS on iPhone & Android
etc. using any free QR code app

Scan to **HEAR** this scale, or go directly
to flametreemusic.com

START
HERE

BASICS

A

A♯/B♭

B

C

C♯/D♭

D

D♯/E♭

E

F

F♯/G♭

G

G♯/A♭

G Mixolydian

This scale works well with: **G**, **G7**, **G9**, **C**, **Gsus2**, **G7sus4 and Dm**
Jeff Beck uses this scale in his 'Freeway Jam' solo.

Scale Notes	Up	G A B C D E F G
	Down	G F E D C B A G

Scan to **HEAR** this scale, or go directly to flametreemusic.com

START HERE

BASICS

A

A#/B♭

B

C

C#/D♭

D

D#/E♭

E

F

F#/G♭

G

G#/A♭

G Wholetone

This scale works well with:
G7♯5, G7♯11, G7♭13, G9♯5 and G13♯5

Scale Notes	Up	G A B C♯ D♯ F G
	Down	G F D♯ C♯ B A G

FREE ACCESS on iPhone & Android
etc. using any free QR code app

Scan to **HEAR** this scale, or go directly
to flametreemusic.com

A♭ Major

This scale works well with:
A♭, A♭maj7, D♭, E♭, B♭m, Fm and Cm

Scale Notes	Up	A♭ B♭ C D♭ E♭ F G A♭
	Down	A♭ G F E♭ D♭ C B♭ A♭

Scan to **HEAR** this scale, or go directly to flametreemusic.com

START HERE

BASICS

A

A♯/B♭

B

C

C♯/D♭

D

D♯/E♭

E

F

F♯/G♭

G

G♯/A♭

A♭ Major Pentatonic

This scale works well with:
A♭, Fm, E♭ and B♭sus2

Scale Notes	Up	A♭ B♭ C E♭ F A♭
	Down	A♭ F E♭ C B♭ A♭

FREE ACCESS on iPhone & Android
etc. using any free QR code app

Scan to **HEAR** this scale, or go directly
to flametreemusic.com

Sidebar navigation:
START HERE
BASICS
A
A#/B♭
B
C
C#/D♭
D
D#/E♭
E
F
F#/G♭
G
G#/A♭

A♭ Lydian

This scale works well with:
A♭, A♭maj7, E♭ and B♭7

Scale Notes	Up	A♭ B♭ C D E♭ F G A♭
	Down	A♭ G F E♭ D C B♭ A♭

G# Natural Minor

START
HERE

BASICS

A

A#/B♭

B

C

C#/D♭

D

D#/E♭

E

F

F#/G♭

G

G#/A♭

This scale works well with:
G#m, G#m7, G#m9 and B

Scale Notes	Up	G# A# B C# D# E F# G#
	Down	G# F# E D# C# B A# G#

Scan to **HEAR** this scale, or go directly
to flametreemusic.com

G♯ Harmonic Minor

This scale works well with:
G♯m, G♯m-maj7, C♯m, D♯7, G♯sus2 and G♯sus4

Scale Notes	Up	G♯ A♯ B C♯ D♯ E F× G♯
	Down	G♯ F× E D♯ C♯ B A♯ G♯

FREE ACCESS on iPhone & Android etc. using any free QR code app

Scan to **HEAR** this scale, or go directly to flametreemusic.com

START HERE

BASICS

A

A♯/B♭

B

C

C♯/D♭

D

D♯/E♭

E

F

F♯/G♭

G

G♯/A♭

G♯ Melodic Minor

This scale works well with:
G♯m, G♯m6, G♯m6/9, G♯m-maj7, D♯7 and G7

Scale Notes	Up	G♯ A♯ B C♯ D♯ E♯ F× G♯
	Down	G♯ F♯ E♮ D♯ C♯ B A♯ G♯

Scan to **HEAR** this scale, or go directly to flametreemusic.com

G♯ Dorian

This scale works well with:
G♯m, G♯m7, A♯m7, G♯sus2 and G♯sus4

Scale Notes	Up	G♯ A♯ B C♯ D♯ E♯ F♯ G♯
	Down	G♯ F♯ E♯ D♯ C♯ B A♯ G♯

Scan to **HEAR** this scale, or go directly to flametreemusic.com

START HERE

BASICS

A

A♯/B♭

B

C

C♯/D♭

D

D♯/E♭

E

F

F♯/G♭

G

G♯/A♭

G♯ Minor Pentatonic

This scale works well with:
G♯m, G♯7, D♯7 and B

Scale Notes		
	Up	G♯ B C♯ D♯ F♯ G♯
	Down	G♯ F♯ D♯ C♯ B G♯

Scan to **HEAR** this scale, or go directly to flametreemusic.com

G♯ Blues

This scale works well with:
G♯7, C♯7 and D♯7

Scale Notes	Up	G♯ B C♯ D♮ D♯ F♯ G♯
	Down	G♯ F♯ D♯ D♮ C♯ B G♯

Scan to **HEAR** this scale, or go directly to flametreemusic.com

START HERE

BASICS

A

A♯/B♭

B

C

C♯/D♭

D

D♯/E♭

E

F

F♯/G♭

G

G♯/A♭

173

A♭ Mixolydian

This scale works well with:

A♭, A♭7, A♭9, D♭, A♭sus2, A♭7sus4 and E♭m

Scale Notes	Up	A♭ B♭ C D♭ E♭ F G♭ A♭
	Down	A♭ G♭ F E♭ D♭ C B♭ A♭

Scan to **HEAR** this scale, or go directly to flametreemusic.com

START HERE

BASICS

A

A#/B♭

B

C

C#/D♭

D

D#/E♭

E

F

F#/G♭

G

G#/A♭

A♭ Wholetone

This scale works well with:
A♭7♯5, A♭7♯11, A♭7♭13, A♭9♯5 and A♭13♯5

Scale Notes	Up	A♭ B♭ C D E G♭ A♭
	Down	A♭ G♭ E D C B♭ A♭

FREE ACCESS on iPhone & Android
etc. using any free QR code app

Scan to **HEAR** this scale, or go directly
to flametreemusic.com

START
HERE

BASICS

A

A♯/B♭

B

C

C♯/D♭

D

D♯/E♭

E

F

F♯/G♭

G

G♯/A♭

flametreemusic.com

The Flame Tree Music website complements our range of print books and offers easy access to chords and scales online, and on the move, through tablets, smartphones, and desktop computers.

1. The site offers access to chord diagrams and finger positions for both the guitar and the piano/keyboard, presenting a wide range of sound options to help develop good listening technique, and to assist you in identifying the chord and each note within it.

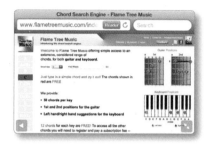

2. The site offers 12 **free** chords, those most commonly used in bands and songwriting.

3. A subscription is available if you'd like the full range of chords, **50** for **each key**.

4. Guitar chords are shown with **first** and **second positions on the fretboard**.

5. For the keyboard, you can **see** and **hear** each note in **left-** and **right-hand positions**.

6. Choose the key, then the chord name from the drop down menu. Note that the **red chords** are available **free**. Those in blue can be accessed with a subscription.

7. Once you've selected the chord, press **GO** and the details of the chord will be shown, with chord spellings, keyboard and guitar fingerings.

8. Sounds are provided in four easy-to-understand configurations.

9. flametreemusic.com also gives you access to **20 scales for each key**.